SOCIAL MEDIA FREE TOOLS

2016 EDITION:

Social Media Marketing Tools to Turbocharge Your Brand for Free on Facebook, LinkedIn, Twitter, YouTube & Every Other Network Known to Man

BY JASON MCDONALD, PH.D.

© SUMMER, 2016, JM INTERNET GROUP

https://www.jm-seo.org/

0
INTRODUCTION

Social Media Marketing is the art and science of nurturing positive buzz about your business on everything from Facebook to LinkedIn, Twitter to Google+, Yelp to Blogs, YouTube to Pinterest, Instagram to Snapchat, and on and on. Social media can be daunting, and there is a burgeoning ecosystem of pricey paid tools. The paid tools can be great, but what's better are **free tools** that are as good, or even better, as pricey paid tools with big ad budgets and smarty pants sales staffs. In the spirit of the cheapest man alive (*ask my children*), this *Social Media Toolbook* (fully updated for Summer, 2016) identifies **free** tools to turbocharge your marketing efforts on every single social media network known to man. (*Well not all of them, but most of them, and all the important ones*). The zero, zip, nada cost tools identified in this *Toolbook* can help you identify social media opportunities, manage your customer relationships, measure your success, get your boss to give you a raise, and give you telepathic powers. (Ok everything but the telepathic powers).

Let's get started!

CONTENTS:

>> How This Toolbook Works

This *Toolbook* is meant as a companion to my online classes in Social Media Marketing at https://www.jm-seo.org/ as well as my book, the *Social Media Marketing Workbook* available for sale on Amazon.com at http://jmlinks.com/smm. It identifies free tools but assumes you have a conceptual framework from my classes (or my books or elsewhere) to create a strategy to market via social media. Like the tools or workout machines in a gym, *these tools are just tools*: they do not do marketing for you but rather help you to do marketing more efficiently. Furthermore, the tools identified in this *Toolbook* are overwhelmingly free, despite the growing list of paid social media tools. After all, a huge part of the attraction of social media is that it is a free, low-cost way to generate positive marketing buzz.

Why use *paid* tools when so many wonderful *free* tools are available?

>> Toolbook Contents

>> Register Your Copy of the Social Media Toolbooks

Why register? Well, by registering you can access this document in **PDF** format on your desktop computer or tablet, making each link "clickable" to the resource identified. Many people buy this book in Kindle format, but it's a bit clunky to click from one of the free tools indicated in the book to the actual tool on the Web using your Kindle, so that's reason #1 to register. It's easier to use it in PDF format.

Reason #2 to register is that you'll get access to my **Dashboards**, which are the best tools laid out for you in easy-to-use format. These are the tools I use on a daily basis as I chart social media marketing success for my clients.

And reason #3? Behind door #3 are **free review copies** of my Workbooks (on SEO and Social Media Marketing) as well as email alerts when we release NEW and UPDATED copies of the Toolbooks.

To register, go to https://www.jm-seo.org/free and sign up for the email mailing list. Members of the email list have permanent access to both the SEO and Social Media Marketing Toolbooks for free!

» MORE FREE STUFF AND IN-DEPTH TRAINING

Want more free stuff? *Gosh you're greedy.* But oh well. Here are links for help and more information:

- Jasonmcdonald.org (https://www.jasonmcdonald.org/) - my personal website, full of SEO, Social Media, and AdWords blog posts, information, and how to contact me with questions, comments, or concerns. Don't hesitate to reach out!
- The JM Internet Group (https://www.jm-seo.org/) - my corporate training site. Don't miss the blog, the free video tutorials, and other free goodies. All have lots of good insights into SEO, AdWords, and Social Media, including many free webinars and resource links.\
- My Q&A blog at http://jm-seotips.org, where I answer incoming questions. Don't be shy: ask one.
- More free stuff at https://www.jm-seo.org/free. Be sure to take the free Webinars and register for my email newsletter on *Serious Humor*!
- The *Social Media Marketing Workbook* available at http://jmlinks.com/smm for sale on Amazon – *ok not free, but useful* (in my humble opinion). Priced at the low low price of $39.99, and watch for sales!

If you are interested in consulting services, in-depth social media marketing training, or just need a friend to talk to, call 800-298-4065 or visit the **JM Internet Group** website above. Consulting, classes, and books are reasonably priced, and designed to help you go from Social Media Marketing zero to hero.

» ACKNOWLEDGEMENTS

A labor of love, this *Toolbook* is also a labor of research, work, curation, editing, and the never-ending search for typos and dead links. Many thanks to Gloria McNabb and Noelle Decambra of the JM Internet Group (*my beloved wife, without whom nothing would ever really get done nor be fun*). My daughter, Ava, inspired me as a budding YouTube star, as well. My daughter, Hannah, who is nearly a Senior in college, inspired me to work long hours to try to pay her college tuition bills. And, of course, many thanks to "Buddy," my fearless Labrador retriever who accompanies me on the highways and byways of the San Francisco Bay Area. Buddy has an unlimited dog toy budget – yet another motivator for my quest to become a successful author. Thanks, everyone!

» COPYRIGHT AND DISCLAIMER

1

CONTENT

Content is king, and queen, and jack! You gotta gotta create content to share: blog posts, images, infographics, memes, and even videos. You can not only get better at creating quality content for social media sharing; you can also monitor and use the content of other folks. Content, after all, is the "fuel" for your social media marketing shares. Rev up your engines (and the engines of other folks, too)!

Here are the best free tools and resources for content marketing!

YOUTUBE CREATOR HUB - http://youtube.com/yt/creators

Help center for those creating YouTube content. Learn how to better edit your videos, get them up on YouTube, etc. Has lessons on growing your audience, boot camp, and how to get viewers and even how to earn money via YouTube.

Rating: 5 Stars | **Category:** resource

FEEDLY - http://feedly.com/

Feedly is a newsreader integrated with Google+ or Facebook. It's useful for social media because you can follow important blogs or other content and share it with your followers. It can also spur great blog ideas.

Rating: 5 Stars | **Category:** resource

BUZZSUMO - http://buzzsumo.com/

Buzzsumo is a 'buzz' monitoring tool for social media. Input a website (domain) and/or a topic and see what people are sharing across Facebook, Twitter, Google+ and other social media. Great for link-building (because what people link to is what they share), and also for social media.

Rating: 5 Stars | **Category:** tool

YOUTUBE TOOLS - http://bitly.com/ytcreatecorner

YouTube has done more and more to make it easier to publish and promote videos. This page lists six tools: YouTube Capture, YouTube Editor, Captions, Audio Library, Slideshow and YouTube Analytics. All of them are fantastic, free tools about YouTube by YouTube.

Rating: 5 Stars | **Category:** resource

PHOTOPIN - http://photopin.com

Get in the habit of creating blog posts with images by using PhotoPin. PhotoPin searches millions of Creative Commons photos and allows you to preview, download any of multiple sizes to upload into your posts, and provides handy cut and paste HTML for attribution, a small price to pay for royalty-free images. Adding images to your blog posts doesn't get any easier than this.

Rating: 4 Stars | **Category:** service

GOOGLE NEWS - https://news.google.com/

Excellent for reputation management as well as keeping up-to-date on specific keywords that matter to you and your business. First, sign in to your Google account or gmail. Second, customize Google news for your interest. Third, monitor your reputation as well as topics that matter to you. Go Google!

Rating: 4 Stars | **Category:** service

TAG BOARD - https://tagboard.com/

Hashtags have moved beyond Twitter. This amazing cool tool allows you to take a hashtag and browse Facebook and Twitter and Instagram, etc., so see posts that relate to that hashtag. Then you can find related tags. Oh, and you can use it as a content discovery tool, too.

Rating: 4 Stars | **Category:** tool

PABLO - https://buffer.com/pablo

Take an image, add some text. Presto! You have an engaging image for your blog post or social sharing. Memes, anyone?

Rating: 4 Stars | **Category:** tool

CREATIVE COMMONS SEARCH - http://search.creativecommons.org

Another resource to find royalty-free images, clip art, sound and music to share or utilize with other content. Great way to find shareable images to embed into blog posts.

Rating: 4 Stars | **Category:** resource

GOOGLE EMAIL ALERTS - https://www.google.com/alerts

Use Google to alert you by email for search results that matter to you. Input your company name, for example, to see when new web pages, blog posts, or other items surface on the web. Enter your target keywords to keep an eye on yourself and your competitors. Part of the Gmail system.

Rating: 4 Stars | **Category:** service

QZZR - https://qzzr.com

Create online quizzes and share with your social network. What cat breed are you? If you were a Twilight character, which character would you be? Fun quizzes to encourage social sharing.

Rating: 4 Stars | **Category:** tool

COMPFIGHT - http://compfight.com

Unclear where the name comes from, but no matter. This incredible tool allows you to search for royalty-based and royalty-free images. Great for finding images for blogging and posting to social media. Quickly locate royalty-free images!

Rating: 4 Stars | **Category:** service

YOUTUBE CAPTURE - https://youtube.com/capture

YouTube Capture is an app for your mobile phone, which makes it easy to capture and edit videos right on your phone. Imagine you are a marketer / retailer and you want to use your phone to easily capture customer interactions, and upload (quickly / easily) to YouTube. Get the picture?

Rating: 4 Stars | **Category:** tool

FOTER - http://foter.com

Add some color (or monochrome) to your blog posts with Foter. Search over 200 million high-quality, free, downloadable stock photos. Don't forget to copy and paste photo attribution credits included with the images details into your blog post.

Rating: 4 Stars | **Category:** resource

MEME GENERATOR - http://memegenerator.net

Memes are shareable photos, usually with text. But how do you create them? Why, use memegenerator.net. Oh, and if you visit this site, you will spend about half an hour just laughing at stupid, funny memes. Now, get back to work, Keanu Reeves.

Rating: 3 Stars | **Category:** tool

PIKIZ - http://getpikiz.com

Take an image, add some text plus a lot of emotion and it might just go viral. This is a free / freemium image maker plus textifier. Memes, anyone?

Rating: 3 Stars | **Category:** tool

MOZ GUIDE TO CONTENT MARKETING - http://bitly.com/mozcontent

MOZ is the producer of fabulous SEO tools. Read this free in-depth guide to CONTENT MARKETING. It is a bit techie, and of course emphasizes SEO.

Rating: 3 Stars | **Category:** resource

DRUMUP - http://drumup.io/

DrumUp discovers and helps you share great content to your social media accounts

so you can start meaningful conversations with your followers. In simple words, it crawls the Web so you don't have to, and then you take that 'scraped' content and can share it to your followers. Efficiency, anyone?

Rating: 3 Stars | **Category:** tool

WINDOWS MOVIE MAKER - http://bitly.com/windowsmov

For those on the Windows platform, Movie Maker is the goto free program to edit videos for YouTube and other platforms.

Rating: 3 Stars | **Category:** tool

EASELY - http://easel.ly

Use thousands of templates and design objects to easily create infographics for your blog.

Rating: 3 Stars | **Category:** tool

ADDICTOMATIC - http://addictomatic.com

Nifty way to enter your company name or keyword and view a 'snapshot' of what's buzzing across multiple popular sources. Most useful for monitoring online reputation, admittedly at a high level of generality.

Rating: 3 Stars | **Category:** tool

RENOUN - http://renoun.io/

Similar to the defunct Topsy, this search engine finds NEW content especially articles on the Internet. You can search by keyword. It also shows you social shares.

Rating: 3 Stars | **Category:** service

EMOTIONAL MARKETING VALUE HEADLINE ANALYZER - http://www.aminstitute.com/headline/

Brought to you by the Advanced Marketing Institute, this tool attempts to analyze the emotional content of your blog post headline. It doesn't seem to work particularly well, because it's hard for computers to get angry or sad or depressed. But - I'm crying as a I write this - it's still worth a try.

Rating: 3 Stars | **Category:** tool

CONTENT MARKETING WORLD - http://www.contentmarketingworld.com/

Content Marketing World is the one event where you can learn and network with the best and the brightest in the content marketing industry. You will leave with all the materials you need to take a content marketing strategy back to your team – and – to implement a content marketing plan that will grow your business and inspire your audience.

Rating: 3 Stars | **Category:** conference

SLIDESHARE - http://www.slideshare.net/

PowerPoint slides for the Web. Create a "deck," upload it to SlideShare and have a) a place to put content in slide format, and b) a platform that can also lead to discoverability. PowerPoint on the Web, PowerPoint gone social.

Rating: 3 Stars | **Category:** tool

SPRUCE - http://www.tryspruce.com/

Take text and add an image. This tool allows you to easily add text to an image; great for social sharing, especially on Facebook. Really easy, really fun, and free.

Rating: 3 Stars | **Category:** tool

WHAT DO YOU LOVE? - http://www.wdyl.com/

Despite its name, What do you love? is really an interesting monitoring service by Google. Type in a keyword that you want to 'monitor' and Google will build out all sorts of searches and monitoring tools. It's very cool, but we're not completely sure why it's called "What do you love?"

Rating: 3 Stars | **Category:** tool

MENTION - https://mention.com/en/

Similar to Google Alerts. Enter your email address and get free email alerts when topics are mentioned. For example, use your company name (personal name) and monitor your reputation online.

Rating: 3 Stars | **Category:** service

YOUTUBE EDITOR - https://www.youtube.com/editor

While there is Microsoft Windows Movie Maker and Apple iMovie, there is also a free YouTube editor for your videos. Not incredibly powerful, but free and easy to use 'in the cloud.'

Rating: 3 Stars | **Category:** tool

PIXABAY - http://pixabay.com

Pixabay is a photo sharing community and a great source of royalty-free, attribution-free, stock images for your blog. Ignore the first row of sponsored images in the search results.

Rating: 3 Stars | **Category:** service

PIKTOCHART - http://piktochart.com

Free infographic creator. Useful for blogging and creating 'link bait' for link building.

Rating: 2 Stars | **Category:** tool

PAPER.LI - http://paper.li/

Create a curated set of content just for your audience. Paper.li is a content platform - you define what you want on a page, and it builds a custom newspaper on the Web for you (and your customers).

Rating: 2 Stars | **Category:** tool

PowToon - http://www.powtoon.com/

PowToon provides animated video production using the freemium pricing model. Play around with it to create animated videos to present anything you want about your business. Paid plans available, but you can do some cool stuff for free.

Rating: 2 Stars | **Category:** tool

INFO.GRAM - https://infogr.am

Another free way to create infographics and charts. Free plan is limited to 10 infographics, 10 uploaded images, no private sharing and no downloads or live connections.

Rating: 2 Stars | **Category:** tool

2

BLOGS

Before there was Social Media, there were Blogs. In many ways, one might argue that Blogs begat the social web. Blogs can be used to enhance your SEO (Search Engine Optimization) strategy, and blogs can be linked with your Facebook, Twitter, and other Social Media marketing efforts. Moreover, comments and conversations allow blogs to be social, and sites like Wordpress (http://www.wordpress.com/), Typepad (http://www.typepad.com/), Tumblr (http://www.tumblr.com/), or Blogger (http://www.blogger.com/) make it easy to start a blog.

Here are the best **free** tools and resources for blogging, ranked with the best first!

BLOG TOPIC GENERATOR - http://hubspot.com/blog-topic-generator

If you're hurting for blog topic ideas, try this fun tool from HubSpot. Enter three nouns, then watch the tool generate a weeks worth of blog topics. If none of the generated topics pique your interest, hit the back key and try, try again until one does.

Rating: 4 Stars | **Category:** tool

TWEAK YOUR BIZ TITLE GENERATOR - http://tweakyourbiz.com/tools/title-generator/index.php

Good blog post TITLES are critical. You should include your keywords for SEO purposes, but add some pizazz, some sex appeal, some please-click-me oomph. This nifty tool gets your ideas flowing for good TITLES.

Rating: 4 Stars | **Category:** tool

CREATIVE COMMONS SEARCH - http://search.creativecommons.org

Another resource to find royalty-free images, clip art, sound and music to share or utilize with other content. Great way to find shareable images to embed into blog posts.

Rating: 4 Stars | **Category:** resource

YOAST - https://yoast.com/

Yoast is the No. 1 recommended SEO plugin for WordPress. Highly recommended, as it adds needed functionality to WordPress such as splitting the TITLE tag from the Post TITLE, META description, and a nice 'focus' tool to analyze how well your post is optimized for on page SEO vs. a target keyword.

Rating: 4 Stars | **Category:** tool

PORTENT CONTENT IDEA GENERATOR - http://portent.com/tools/title-maker

Very fun and mind-provocative tool for content ideas and better blog titles. Enter some keywords and the tool will generate some funny titles. So start with keywords and then generate your amazingly, funny and hypnotic blog titles. These then become the HEADLINES on Google by which you can attract more clicks!

Rating: 4 Stars | **Category:** tool

THE HEMINGWAY APP - http://www.hemingwayapp.com/

Let's face it. Americans, and people everywhere, aren't getting smarter. This app allows you to paste in text from your blog post or email, and check the 'grade level.' It also identifies hard-to-read sentences. Can you say DUM IT DOWNE?

Rating: 4 Stars | **Category:** tool

ICEROCKET - http://www.icerocket.com/

IceRocket is a very good blog search engine. Don't miss the Trend Tool that allows you to enter a keyword and watch trends.

Rating: 4 Stars | **Category:** engine

SIMPLE GUIDE TO BUSINESS BLOGGING - http://simplybusiness.co.uk/microsites/guide-business-blogging

Interactive step-by-step guide to business blogging. Comprised of key questions and linked resources from around the web with more information. Thoughtful and well constructed.

Rating: 4 Stars | **Category:** resource

PHOTOPIN - http://photopin.com

Get in the habit of creating blog posts with images by using PhotoPin. PhotoPin searches millions of Creative Commons photos and allows you to preview, download any of multiple sizes to upload into your posts, and provides handy cut and paste HTML for attribution, a small price to pay for royalty-free images. Adding images to your blog posts doesn't get any easier than this.

Rating: 4 Stars | **Category:** service

WORDPRESS PLUGIN DIRECTORY - http://wordpress.org/plugins

WordPress is the most popular blogging platform. This is their complete directory of plugins. Don't forget to install an SEO plugin to improve your searchability!

Rating: 4 Stars | **Category:** resource

FOTER - http://foter.com

Add some color (or monochrome) to your blog posts with Foter. Search over 200 million high-quality, free, downloadable stock photos. Don't forget to copy and paste photo attribution credits included with the images details into your blog post.

Rating: 4 Stars | **Category:** resource

FACEBOOK COMMENTS PLUGIN -
https://developers.facebook.com/docs/plugins/comments

Want more comments on your blog? Want people who comment to have those comments go viral? This Facebook Plugin makes it easy for people to comment on your blog, no more annoying double registration, plus if they comment you can encourage them to post the comment to their Facebook page - hence, viral marketing!

Rating: 4 Stars | **Category:** tool

BLOG POST HEADLINE ANALYZER - http://coschedule.com/headline-analyzer

Want to write better blog headlines? Use the Blog Post Headline Analyzer to get a feel for how effective your blog post headlines are. This tool analyzes entered headlines across numerous criteria including keywords, sentiment, structure, grammar, and readability to produce a headline score in an attractive graphical format. Try it and see.

Rating: 4 Stars | **Category:** tool

WORD TO CLEAN HTML - https://word2cleanhtml.com/

If you write in Microsoft Word, and then copy / paste into your blog, you'll get insane formatting in the HTML. Thanks Microsoft! Just what we needed: a more bloated web. No worries, Word To Clean HTML to the rescue. Copy into this tool, and it removes the crazy embedded formating.

Rating: 4 Stars | **Category:** tool

COMPFIGHT - http://compfight.com

Unclear where the name comes from, but no matter. This incredible tool allows you to search for royalty-based and royalty-free images. Great for finding images for blogging and posting to social media. Quickly locate royalty-free images!

Rating: 4 Stars | **Category:** service

DRAGON DICTATION - http://bit.ly/dragdictate

This is not a free tool, but it is so useful for blogging that it deserves an 'honorable mention.' Download and install, and you can simple TALK to your computer. Unlike free programs such as those available in Windows, the dictation engine is pretty good 'out of the box' at recognizing speech. Makes blog post writing as easy as talking to your computer!

Rating: 4 Stars | **Category:** tool

LINKEDIN PULSE - https://www.linkedin.com/pulse/

Need ideas for your next blog post? Look no further than LinkedIn Pulse where top business influencers post their thoughts daily. Even better, you can post to LinkedIin Pulse and become a LinkedIn superstar as well. Even even better: post to both LinkedIn Pulse and your own blog.

Rating: 4 Stars | **Category:** resource

PIXABAY - http://pixabay.com

Pixabay is a photo sharing community and a great source of royalty-free, attribution-free, stock images for your blog. Ignore the first row of sponsored images in the search results.

Rating: 3 Stars | **Category:** service

COPYSCAPE - http://copyscape.com

Since Google can penalize websites with plagiarized content, avoid being penalized for someone stealing your content with Copyscape. Enter the page URL and Copyscape will return pages which may have duplicated its content. Copyscape even provides some tips and resources should content have been plagiarized.

Rating: 3 Stars | **Category:** tool

READABILITY TESTER - http://read-able.com/

Has anyone ever told you you should write your blog on the '4th grade level?' or the 6th grade level? Or Ph.D. level? Well, OK, not for Ph.D's. This tool allows you to input your web address and/or paste in some content and see what level it's at.

Rating: 3 Stars | **Category:** tool

GUEST BLOG POST OPPORTUNITY FINDER - http://mangiamarketing.com/free-link-building-tools/guest-post-opportunity-finder

This nifty little tool takes your keywords and creates Google searches to help you find guest blogging opportunities.

Rating: 3 Stars | **Category:** tool

CONTENT MARKETING GENERATOR - http://bit.ly/contentgen

From Online Ventures Group: input your target customer or reader, plus an idea and it generates a barage of blog headlines or blog ideas. No more writer's block!

Rating: 3 Stars | **Category:** tool

WORDPRESS SUPPORT - http://wordpress.org/support

WordPress is the No. 1 blogging platform but it is anything but simple or intuitive. Use the support site to 'get started' with WordPress as a blogging platform, as well as to learn the more esoteric elements of WordPress.

Rating: 3 Stars | **Category:** resource

EMOTIONAL MARKETING VALUE HEADLINE ANALYZER - http://www.aminstitute.com/headline/

Brought to you by the Advanced Marketing Institute, this tool attempts to analyze the emotional content of your blog post headline. It doesn't seem to work particularly well, because it's hard for computers to get angry or sad or depressed. But - I'm crying as a I write this - it's still worth a try.

Rating: 3 Stars | **Category:** tool

RHYMEZONE - http://www.rhymezone.com/

Sometimes, it's true you need glue for your blog, or just a nog. If it's that, or if it's a cat, you need to know where this is at. RhymeZone is run by gnomes, and knows how it goes when it's time to rhyme you need RhymeZone so your blog isn't lost in the fog.

Rating: 3 Stars | **Category:** tool

SPRUCE - http://www.tryspruce.com/

Take text and add an image. This tool allows you to easily add text to an image; great for social sharing, especially on Facebook. Really easy, really fun, and free.

Rating: 3 Stars | **Category:** tool

WORDPRESS SEO TUTORIAL - http://yoast.com/articles/wordpress-seo

This is a very good guide for WordPress SEO using the Yoast plugin. It covers only the technical issues, however, but when combined with our classes and an understanding of keyword research, website structure, and off-page SEO link building - this guide is very helpful for crossing the t's and dotting the i's of a strong SEO-friendly WordPress website.

Rating: 3 Stars | **Category:** resource

ULTIMATE HEADLINE FORMULAS

SAVE TIME ON SOCIAL MEDIA WITH BUFFER. SCHEDULE YOUR FIRST POST NOW!

ULTIMATE HEADLINE FORMULAS - https://blog.bufferapp.com/headline-formulas

If you've wondered how to create headlines for blog posts, articles, emails, etc., which will entice readers to click and read on, this article gathers a gaggle of formulas from some of the best sources for headline writing in one place. It also includes a free, downloadable PDF of the best headline formulas.

Rating: 3 Stars | **Category:** article

PITCHERIFIC - https://pitcherific.com/

Blogging is a lot like 'pitching' clients. You need a good headline, an angle on why this is important, often you are 'solving' a 'problem' with a 'solution.' This fun tool will help you devise a pitch, which could also become a great blog post.

Rating: 3 Stars | **Category:** tool

WORD COUNTER - https://wordcounter.net/

Counts words and characters. Useful for SEO, especially TITLE and META DESCRIPTION tags for which limited characters are displayed in search results.

Rating: 3 Stars | **Category:** tool

BLOGGER - https://www.blogger.com/

Need a blog? Google's Blogger platform, sometimes referred to as Blogspot, while not as pervasive as WordPress, is quick, easy, and very SEO friendly. If you want a straightforward, hosted, business blog, Blogger might be a better choice than WordPress.com. You can even attach a domain!

Rating: 3 Stars | **Category:** service

CLICHÉ FINDER - http://www.westegg.com/cliche/

Make your writing more interesting! Use more exclamation marks! Sound witty and sound stupid all at the same time! Enter the Cliché Finder. Enter some words, and it identifies common cliches on the topic.

Rating: 2 Stars | **Category:**

HEADLINE GENERATOR - http://internetmarketingcourse.com/freeheadlinegenerator

Got writer's block? Wondering how to generate a snazzy headline for a product page, blog post, or even news release? Answer a few questions about your blog post or product page, and this tool will generate a list of suggested headlines.

Rating: 2 Stars | **Category:** tool

FLICKR ADVANCED SEARCH - https://www.flickr.com/search/advanced/

Yet another way to find royalty-free images for your blog. Flickr Advanced Search.

Rating: 2 Stars | **Category:** service

TWITTERFEED - http://twitterfeed.com

Feed your blog to Twitter, Facebook, LinkedIn and other social networks, automagically.

Rating: 2 Stars | **Category:** service

3

FACEBOOK

Facebook (https://www.facebook.com/) is the largest Social Media website on the planet. Facebook fits into what I call the "My Friends" category - friends post to Facebook, friends read what friends post, friends meet friends through friends, friends play games with friends... And sometimes friends connect with companies, or "pages" in the lingo of Facebook. Set up a company **page** on Facebook, and begin to market via friends, family, and fun. Note: these days, unfortunately, a certain amount of advertising can be a necessary for success at Facebook marketing! (Thanks Zuckerberg!)

At any rate, here are the best **free** resources for Facebook marketing, ranked with the best first!

FACEBOOK HELP CENTER - http://facebook.com/help

The 'missing' help pages on Facebook. Useful for learning everything on the king of social media. Links on advertising, business accounts, connect, Facebook places and more.

Rating: 5 Stars | **Category:** overview

FACEBOOK SOCIAL PLUGINS (LIKE BOXES AND BUTTONS) - http://developers.facebook.com/docs/plugins

Make it easy for your Facebook fans and fans-to-be to 'like' your company and Facebook pages you create. The best Facebook resource for all plugins to integrate Facebook with your website, including the Like, Share & Send Button, Comments, Follow Button and others.

Rating: 5 Stars | **Category:** tool

FACEBOOK LIKE BUTTON FOR WEB - https://developers.facebook.com/docs/plugins/like-button

The Facebook Like button lets a user share your content with friends on Facebook. When the user clicks the Like button on your site, a story appears in the user's friends' News Feeds with a link back to your website.

Rating: 5 Stars | **Category:** tool

TAG BOARD - https://tagboard.com/

Hashtags have moved beyond Twitter. This amazing cool tool allows you to take a hashtag and browse Facebook and Twitter and Instagram, etc., so see posts that relate to that hashtag. Then you can find related tags. Oh, and you can use it as a content discovery tool, too.

Rating: 4 Stars | **Category:** tool

SHORTSTACK - http://www.shortstack.com/

ShortStack is a nifty program to optimize your social media campaigns on platforms like Facebook, Twitter, Instagram and Pinterest. On Facebook, ShortStack provides polls and surveys, contents, and forms for newsletter signups, contact us, etc. and is free for Business Pages up to a certain number of Likes. No expiring trials. No credit card required.

Rating: 4 Stars | **Category:** service

KEYHOLE - http://keyhole.co

This tool provides real-time social conversation tracking for Twitter, Facebook, and Instagram. Use this tool to measure conversations around your business, identify prospective clients and influencers talking about your services, and find relevant content. Enables tracking of hashtags, keywords, and URLs.

Rating: 4 Stars | **Category:** tool

FACEBOOK ADVERTISING - http://facebook.com/advertising

Facebook advertising opportunities. Run text ads on Facebook by selecting the demographics of who you want to reach. Pay-per-click model.

Rating: 4 Stars | **Category:** overview

SOCIALOOMPH - https://www.socialoomph.com/

SocialOomph is a powerful free (and paid) suite of tools to manage and schedule your Twitter and Facebook posts. Imagine going to the beach, forgetting about the office, yet having 67 different Tweets auto-posted...that's what SocialOomph is about. Use technology to appear busy and Facebooking / Tweeting all the time.

Rating: 4 Stars | **Category:** tool

IFTTT - https://ifttt.com

This app, If Then Then That, is a great tool for linking multiple social media accounts. It allows you to create 'recipes' that link your tools exactly the way you like them! For example: make a recipe that adds to a Google Apps spreadsheet every time a particular user uploads to Instagram - a great way to keep up with your competitors SMM strategies! With over 120 supported applications, the 'recipes' are endless, making this a good tool for your SMM strategies.

Rating: 4 Stars | **Category:** tool

FACEBOOK PAGE BASICS (FOR BUSINESS) -
https://www.facebook.com/business/learn/facebook-page-basics

Confused by Facebook for Business? Have no fear, Learn How, Facebook's online learning center for businesses, is here. This easy-to-use resource, complete with videos, images and step-by-step instructions, answers businesses' frequently asked questions, like how to create a Page, and how to create a Custom Audience. Learn How content is organized to be flexible: use it in-depth, or as a reference library as questions arise.

Rating: 4 Stars | **Category:** tutorial

FACEBOOK FOR BUSINESS: MARKETING SOLUTIONS -
https://www.facebook.com/marketing

Official pages on Facebook-approved 'best practices' for marketing your company on Facebook.

Rating: 4 Stars | **Category:** overview

SMALL BUSINESS GUIDE TO FACEBOOK -
http://simplybusiness.co.uk/microsites/facebook-for-small-businesses

Interactive step-by-step flowchart to using Facebook for small business. Comprised of key questions and linked resources with more information. Chart is divided into different areas including goals and measurement, engagement, page management, Facebook ads, and advanced tips. Worth a look.

Rating: 4 Stars | **Category:** resource

LIKEALYZER - http://likealyzer.com

LikeAlyzer analyzes the Facebook Page you enter and provides a very simple, easy to read report even the most statistically averse will understand. Best of all,

LikeAlyzer provides an overall score and recommendations on where/how to improve. Recommendations are customized and analysis is based on the metrics the company has found to be important: presence, dialogue, action and information.

Rating: 4 Stars | **Category:** tool

FACEBOOK PAGES HELP CENTER - https://facebook.com/help/281592001947683

Here it is. The help center for Facebook 'pages', where businesses, organizations, and brands live. Use this handy dandy resource from Facebook to answer your most basic questions - such as how to set up a page for a business, how to administer your page (e.g., comments, kicking users off and all that fun stuff), as well as how to manage admins. It is the first 'goto' page for help with Facebook Pages for business.

Rating: 4 Stars | **Category:** resource

TAGBOARD - http://tagboard.com

Hashtags started on Twitter, but now they are everywhere. Use this tool to research existing hashtags across a variety of social media, including Twitter, Facebook, Google+, Instagram, Flickr, Vine, and define your own. Fun and informative, too.

Rating: 3 Stars | **Category:** service

WOOBOX - http://woobox.com/

Create coupons, sweepstakes, photo contests, polls, and custom Facebook tabs to woo your fans. Simply, the most viral features anywhere for the best price. Facebook tabs for Twitter, Instagram, Pinterest, and Google+, it's all here.

Rating: 3 Stars | **Category:** vendor

TWITTER TAB ON FACEBOOK - https://apps.facebook.com/twitter-tab-app

This slick little app allows you to easily add your Twitter feed to your Facebook page as a tab. You can also do this for Instagram and a Pinterest. It's very, very easy, and free!

Rating: 3 Stars | **Category:** service

DRUMUP - http://drumup.io/

DrumUp discovers and helps you share great content to your social media accounts

so you can start meaningful conversations with your followers. In simple words, it crawls the Web so you don't have to, and then you take that 'scraped' content and can share it to your followers. Efficiency, anyone?

Rating: 3 Stars | **Category:** tool

FACEBOOK BOOST YOUR POSTS -
https://www.facebook.com/business/help/547448218658012

Not a free tool in any way shape or form, but still important. A boosted post is way to jump to the head of the Facebook line. Separate yourself from a little cash, and get Facebook to 'promote' your post to your fans a little longer, a little more prominently.

Rating: 3 Stars | **Category:** service

FACEBOOK AWARDS - https://www.facebook-studio.com/awards/about

If need some creative inspiration for your Facebook business page, peruse the Facebook Awards. These awards, established by Facebook, celebrate the best creative work on the social network, as chosen by some of the top creatives in the industry. Not only do they recognize excellence in execution, they set the bar for creative growth and evolution on Facebook. Check them and see!

Rating: 3 Stars | **Category:** resource

FACEBOOK PAGE RANKING - https://www.quintly.com/facebook-page-ranking/

This nifty tool helps you find the highest ranked pages in any one of dozens of Facebook categories and allows you to sort them by number of Likes, People Talking About This and net and percent change for these statistics over the last 30 days.

Rating: 3 Stars | **Category:** resource

SPRUCE - http://www.tryspruce.com/

Take text and add an image. This tool allows you to easily add text to an image; great for social sharing, especially on Facebook. Really easy, really fun, and free.

Rating: 3 Stars | **Category:** tool

PINVOLVE - http://www.pinvolve.co/

This tool automatically syncs your Facebook and Pinterest pages, allowing you to integrate your social media marketing strategies. Free for one Facebook page with limited pinning.

Rating: 2 Stars | **Category:** tool

FANPAGE KARMA - http://fanpagekarma.com

Fanpage Karma is another Facebook Page analytics tool, providing all sorts of valuable information like growth, engagement, service and response time, and of course Karma (a weighted engagement value). Free plan provides reports for only one page, along with limited features.

Rating: 2 Stars | **Category:** tool

HEYO - http://heyo.com/

Yet another tool to create contests and what not for Facebook.

Rating: 2 Stars | **Category:** service

FACEBOOK TIMELINE COVER BANNER - http://timelinecoverbanner.com

Use this online tool to design and create a custom Facebook cover image for your business or personal Facebook page.

Rating: 2 Stars | **Category:** tool

PINTEREST FACEBOOK PAGE TAB - http://woobox.com/pinterest

This tool allows you to add a Pinterest tab to your Facebook page; another great way to integrate your social media marketing strategies! Get complete stats for page views, visits, and likes, segmented by fans and non-fans who view your Facebook page tab.

Rating: 2 Stars | **Category:** tool

FACEBOOK TIMELINE CONTEST - http://contest.agorapulse.com/

Use this nifty free tool to create Facebook Timeline contests and engage fans. The tool lets you create three types of contests: sweepstakes, quizzes, and photo contests, and automatically selects the winner based on the type, thereby saving valuable time. Worth a look.

Rating: 2 Stars | **Category:** tool

PAGEMODO - http://www.pagemodo.com/

Pagemodo is an online tool which enables businesses and Facebook Page owners to design and build their own customized Facebook pages, including cover photos, contests, custom tabs, designing and scheduling posts, and Facebook Ads. Limited functionality available with free account, pay more for additional features.

Rating: 2 Stars | **Category:** tool

FACEBOOK FOR BUSINESS (ADS) - https://facebook.com/business

Facebook's resource hub for business has been refreshed, with a streamlined layout and new content that shows how businesses use Facebook to drive business goals. It includes customer success stories and the latest Facebook marketing news, though is quite salesy, so view with healthy dose of corporate skepticism.

Rating: 2 Stars | **Category:** resource

FACEBOOK GRID TOOL - https://www.facebook.com/ads/tools/text_overlay

If you're going to advertise on Facebook, the amount of text an image can have is limited to 20%. This tool will measure that for you, to ensure your image will be accepted by Facebook. Are these people control freaks or what?

Rating: 2 Stars | **Category:** tool

FANGAGER - http://www.fangager.com/site/

Service providing Facebook fan analytics, management, and engagement tools. With it, you can not only identify top fans, but can create activities (e.g., posting, commenting, liking, tweeting) or contests with rewards (e.g., badges, virtual gifts, or real prizes) to boost fan interaction.

Rating: 2 Stars | **Category:** service

4

LINKEDIN

LinkedIn (https://www.linkedin.com/) is the professional business network to Facebook's friend free-for-all. LinkedIn is your on-going office cocktail party, or trade show get together. You can attempt to meet new people directly, but better yet you can leverage existing contacts to meet new contacts (a la six degrees of separation). Your company can use LinkedIn as a recruiting tool, while your sales staff can use it to identify and connect with potential customers.

Here are the best **free** tools and resources for LinkedIn marketing, ranked with the best first!

LINKEDIN HELP CENTER - https://www.linkedin.com/help/linkedin

Learn about all the different features on LinkedIn. From a brief overview to detailed tips, you'll find them here. Learn about profiles. Find out how to get a new job. Use LinkedIn on your mobile phone. Learn how to build your network. Get answers to your questions with Answers.

Rating: 5 Stars | **Category:** overview

SMALL BUSINESS GUIDE TO LINKEDIN -
http://simplybusiness.co.uk/microsites/linkedin-guide

Interactive step-by-step guide to using LinkedIn for small business. Comprised of key questions and linked resources from around the web with more information. Follow this step-by-step guide and make LinkedIn an effective part of your marketing strategy.

Rating: 4 Stars | **Category:** resource

LINKEDIN ENGINEERING - http://engineering.linkedin.com

LinkedIn Engineering hosts a small set of projects and experimental features built by the employees of LinkedIn. Some of these plugins can be good for your LinkedIn marketing efforts.

Rating: 4 Stars | **Category:** tool

LINKEDIN LEARNING WEBINARS -
http://help.linkedin.com/app/answers/detail/a_id/530

LinkedIn hosts live learning webinars on a variety of timely LinkedIn topics. Alternatively, users can view pre-recorded sessions. Topics are designed for a variety of audiences including, job seekers, corporate communications professionals, and journalists.

Rating: 4 Stars | **Category:** resource

OFFICIAL LINKEDIN BLOG - http://blog.linkedin.com

The official LinkedIn Blog...lots of detailed information on what's happening when, where, and how on LinkedIn by LinkedIn staff.

Rating: 4 Stars | **Category:** blog

RAPPORTIVE - http://rapportive.com

Rapportive is a Gmail plugin that works with LinkedIn (and other social media sites). So when you're exchanging email with someone, you can see their LinkedIn profile details. It's sort of a bye-bye privacy app that helps you know how 'important' someone is with whom you are interacting.

Rating: 4 Stars | **Category:** tool

LINKEDIN YOUTUBE CHANNEL - https://www.youtube.com/user/LinkedIn

LinkedIn has some novel advertising opportunities. This is their official YouTube channel. It's pretty salesy, but has some useful information especially on marketing and sales aspects of LinkedIn.

Rating: 4 Stars | **Category:** video

LINKEDIN PULSE - https://www.linkedin.com/pulse/

Need ideas for your next blog post? Look no further than LinkedIn Pulse where top business influencers post their thoughts daily. Even better, you can post to LinkedIin Pulse and become a LinkedIn superstar as well. Even even better: post to both LinkedIn Pulse and your own blog.

Rating: 4 Stars | **Category:** resource

LINKEDIN COMPANY PAGES FAQ - http://linkd.in/1BbOokZ

Interested in setting up a business page on LinkedIn? Here's the official FAQ on LinkedIn company pages.

Rating: 4 Stars | **Category:** resource

FIVE HUNDRED PLUS - http://www.fivehundredplus.com/

Five Hundred Plus is an application that uses LinkedIn to help you make the most of your most valuable connections. You may have heard of Customer Relationship Management (CRM) applications used by companies to manage clients and leads. Five Hundred Plus is inspired by those tools but focuses on your own personal network, not your company's.

Rating: 3 Stars | **Category:** tool

SLIDESHARE - http://www.slideshare.net/

PowerPoint slides for the Web. Create a "deck," upload it to SlideShare and have a) a place to put content in slide format, and b) a platform that can also lead to discoverability. PowerPoint on the Web, PowerPoint gone social.

Rating: 3 Stars | **Category:** tool

LINKEDIN MOBILE - https://mobile.linkedin.com/

LinkedIn has just a few tools, but if you are a power LinkedIn user, these tools can help you search LinkedIn from your Google toolbar, import your contacts and perform other functions to help leverage your network for LinkedIn marketing. Primarily for your phone.

Rating: 3 Stars | **Category:** tool

LINKEDIN ON TWITTER - https://twitter.com/LinkedIn

Yes, LinkedIn is on Twitter. So follow LinkedIn on Twitter for instant updates on LinkedIn about LinkedIn.

Rating: 3 Stars | **Category:** resource

LINKEDIN SHOWCASE PAGES - http://linkd.in/11NWFJd

Finally! LinkedIn has added some clever functionality to brand pages on LinkedIn. You can add a 'Showcase' page that might be a specific product line, theme, or topic. Then this 'page' can share information with followers just like a complete page. Great if your business has individual product lines or topics.

Rating: 3 Stars | **Category:** tool

EXPORT LINKEDIN CONNECTIONS - https://www.linkedin.com/addressBookExport

If you have built up a huge list of LinkedIn connections, use this tool to export them. Backup has never been cooler.

Rating: 3 Stars | **Category:** tool

LINKEDIN ON FACEBOOK - http://facebook.com/LinkedIn

Is LinkedIn on Facebook? Doesn't that sound crazy? Connect with LinkedIn on Facebook for the funner side of business networking at the official LinkedIn page on Facebook.

Rating: 3 Stars | **Category:** resource

LINKEDIN PLUGINS - http://developer.linkedin.com/plugins

Want to cross-promote your LinkedIn page from your website? Here's how. Use this page to find the nifty, official LinkedIn plugins. Share on LinkedIn, or follow us on LinkedIn. If you are in HR, you can even have an 'apply' via LinkedIn button. Cool!

Rating: 3 Stars | **Category:** tool

LINKEDIN MARKETING & ADVERTISING SOLUTIONS - http://business.linkedin.com/marketing-solutions

LinkedIn advertising, like Facebook advertising and unlike Google AdWords, is demographically based. Identify your target customer based on gender, interests, groups they belong to, etc., then set up your pay-per-click advertising.

Rating: 3 Stars | **Category:** service

5

GOOGLE+

Google+ is the one of the newer kid (some would say one of the more *troubled* kids) on the Social Media Marketing block. Guess what? The new kid has a very rich and powerful daddy: Google. Google+ excels at merging social media and SEO; if showing up at the top of a Google search (especially a local search) is important to you, Google+ is the place for you! Check Google+ out at https://plus.google.com/.

Here are the best **free** tools and resources for Google+ marketing, ranked with the best first!

GOOGLE MY BUSINESS (GOOGLE LOCAL / GOOGLE PLACES) -
https://business.google.com/

> Google My Business is the new official name, but behind-the-scenes they still call it Google Places or Google Local or Google+ Local. Or whatchamacallit. This is the official entry point to find and claim your small business listing on Google's local service.
>
> **Rating:** 5 Stars | **Category:** resource

GOOGLE MY BUSINESS (GOOGLE+ LOCAL / GOOGLE PLACES) HELP CENTER -
https://support.google.com/business#topic=4539639

> A wonderful and rather hidden microsite in the Googleplex with many help topics to learn about, modify, and update your Google+ Local listings. Google Local begot Google Places begot Google+ Local begot Google My Business. You and I both wish Google would settle on a name for its local service!
>
> **Rating:** 5 Stars | **Category:** resource

GOOGLE+ REVIEW LINK GENERATOR - https://www.grade.us/home/labs/google-review-link-generator

> Lost as to how to find your company's Google+ reviews? Use this nifty tool to find the exact URL for your reviews. You can also use this to give to clients, directly.
>
> **Rating:** 5 Stars | **Category:** tool

GOOGLE+ PAGE SEARCH - http://www.gpluspagesearch.com/

> Use this nifty site to find competitor Google+ pages easily. Just enter a competitor name (or your own business name), and this search engine will identify the relevant Google+ page.
>
> **Rating:** 5 Stars | **Category:** tool

SMALL BUSINESS GUIDE TO GOOGLE+ -
http://simplybusiness.co.uk/microsites/googleplus-for-small-businesses

Interactive step-by-step flowchart to using Google+ for small business. Comprised of key questions and linked resources with more information. Chart is divided into different areas including set up, integration, and engagement. Worth a look.

Rating: 4 Stars | **Category:** resource

GOOGLE+ BADGE - https://developers.google.com/+/web/badge

This page explains how to add a Google+ badge to your website. Similar, we think, to the Facebook Like button or Like box, this feature will allow users to directly add your page to their Google+ account.

Rating: 4 Stars | **Category:** service

GOOGLE+ +1 BUTTON - https://developers.google.com/+/web/+1button

The Google+ +1 button allows users to 'vote' that your page is cool and important, and they can share it across Google+. This document is intended for webmasters and programmers who want to add and customize the +1 button for their website. Customizations range from simply changing the button's size to advanced loading techniques.

Rating: 4 Stars | **Category:** service

OFFICIAL GOOGLE SOCIAL MEDIA - http://www.google.com/press/google-directory.html

Does Google use Social Media? Of course, it does. Whatever Google product you are into (SEO, AdWords, G+), you can identify the blog, the YouTube channel, the Twitter, etc., of your Google product. Follow Google on social media.

Rating: 4 Stars | **Category:** resource

TAGBOARD - http://tagboard.com

Hashtags started on Twitter, but now they are everywhere. Use this tool to research existing hashtags across a variety of social media, including Twitter,

Facebook, Google+, Instagram, Flickr, Vine, and define your own. Fun and informative, too.

Rating: 3 Stars | **Category:** service

GOOGLE+ WIDGET - http://widgetsplus.com

Are you, or your company, REALLY active on Google+? This nifty widget will stream your posts to your web page or blog, allowing users to see your posts and hopefully decide to follow you on Google+.

Rating: 3 Stars | **Category:** tool

ALL MY + STATISTICS - http://www.allmyplus.com/

This third-party tool helps you analyze what, if anything, is going on in your Google+ account. Make the stark interface more understandable by clicking the 'more info' links to display helpful explanations for each function.

Rating: 3 Stars | **Category:** tool

CIRCLECOUNT - http://www.circlecount.com/

Interesting statistical tool which analyzes your Google+ Profile and Pages in addition to providing a wealth of general Google+ usage information including users with highly engaging content, most followed profiles, most followed pages, to name just a few.

Rating: 3 Stars | **Category:** tool

STEADY DEMAND - http://www.steadydemand.com/

Steady Demand provides free analysis of your Google+ page. Enter your Google+ page ID (e.g., +Jm-seoOrg) and receive a report consisting of Google+ Page analysis and Post analysis. Page analysis assesses your page on about 6 criteria, while the Post analysis presents some aggregate statistics along with a detailed assessment of your last 10 posts. Helpful but not earth shattering.

Rating: 3 Stars | **Category:** tool

CHROME DO SHARE - https://chrome.google.com/webstore/detail/do-share/oglhhmnmdocfhmhlekfdecokagmbchnf

Allows you to schedule posts to personal profiles on Google+, something not easily done with other plugins or applications.

Rating: 3 Stars | **Category:** tool

FRIENDS+ME - https://friendsplus.me

This nifty tool allows you to share your Google+ post to other social networks such as Facebook or Twitter.

Rating: 3 Stars | **Category:** tool

GOOGLE+ SEARCH - https://plus.google.com/people

Beyond just searching plus.google.com, you can use this feature 'inside' of Google+ to find people, pages and posts that might be interesting. Curious how hard Google has made Google+ to search, isn't it? That's just weird, but this is how you can search for people on G+.

Rating: 3 Stars | **Category:** tool

GOOGLE+ HELP CENTER - THE NEW GOOGLE+ - https://support.google.com/plus

Already lost? Here is the official Google+ support pages, focused mainly on users of Google+. But, as a business, these help pages give good insights into how your customer might use Google+. Make sure to be a user of Google+ as well as a producer - and here's where you go to learn how to use Google+.

Rating: 3 Stars | **Category:** resource

GOOGLE+ RECOMMENDED USERS - http://www.recommendedusers.com/

Think no one is on Google+? That there's nothing fun under the sun? Think again. Use this site to find the cool, fun, cognoscenti in the world of Google+.

Rating: 3 Stars | **Category:** resource

GPLUS.TO - GOOGLE PLUS URL SHORTENER - http://gplus.to

Need a nifty short Google-looking URL for your Google+ account? This service - not affiliated with Google+ - may be your answer.

Rating: 1 Stars | **Category:** service

6

PINTEREST

Pin it to win it! If your demographic is female, female shoppers, shoppers in general, idea-seekers in a visual sense, do-it-yourselfers, craftsy types, or men who need toys for their new black lab puppy (that would be me), Pinterest (https://www.pinterest.com/) may be your best performing social media. Online retailers adore this one.

Here are the best free tools and resources for marketing via Pinterest!

PINTEREST ANALYTICS - https://business.pinterest.com/en/pinterest-analytics

Use this tool to easily see what people like from your Pinterest profile and what they pin from your website. Learn about your audience by viewing metrics and common interests. Great tool to analyze your Pinterest marketing strategy.

Rating: 4 Stars | **Category:** tool

PINTEREST GOODIES - https://about.pinterest.com/en/browser-button

Made more for the end user than the business user, this is a resource by Pinterest about Pinterest. For example, both the iOS and Android apps are available here. Don't miss the 'Pin It' button which makes it easy to pin content from your browser, as well as widgets for your website to encourage Pinterest.

Rating: 4 Stars | **Category:** tool

PINTEREST PIN IT BUTTON - https://business.pinterest.com/en/pin-it-button

Want your business to be discovered on Pinterest? The Pin It button allows your customers to save what they like to Pinterest and shows their followers what they're interested in. An easy way to get referral traffic and what Pinterest calls, 'a button that works for you'.

Rating: 4 Stars | **Category:** tool

PINTEREST TOOLS FOR BUSINESS - https://business.pinterest.com/en/tools

Yes, you wanted it. Yes, they created it: a one-stop resource of tools to help your business succeed on Pinterest. Has not only official Pinterest tools, but also a compilation of third party business-friendly tools to help you pin it, to win it.

Rating: 4 Stars | **Category:** tool

PINTEREST RICH PINS - https://business.pinterest.com/rich-pins

Rich Pins are pins that include extra information on the pin itself. The six types of rich pins are: app, movie, recipe, article, product, and place. Use these six rich pins in addition to your 'pin it' link to further enhance your post for your viewers.

Rating: 4 Stars | **Category:** tool

IFTTT - https://ifttt.com

This app, If Then Then That, is a great tool for linking multiple social media accounts. It allows you to create 'recipes' that link your tools exactly the way you like them! For example: make a recipe that adds to a Google Apps spreadsheet every time a particular user uploads to Instagram - a great way to keep up with your competitors SMM strategies! With over 120 supported applications, the 'recipes' are endless, making this a good tool for your SMM strategies.

Rating: 4 Stars | **Category:** tool

CANVA - https://canva.com

This free image editing tool is optimized for Pinterest so all of your pins and boards look sleek. Also has an iPad app.

Rating: 3 Stars | **Category:** tool

PINGROUPIE - http://pingroupie.com

Use this tool to find group boards on Pinterest where you can join and contribute. Additionally, PinGroupie has options for sorting boards by popularity so you can quickly see those with the biggest following, or most pins or likes.

Rating: 3 Stars | **Category:** tool

PINTEREST HELP CENTER - https://help.pinterest.com/en

Need help? Well, guess what, Pinterest has a robust help section, mainly for users but useful for you as a business marketer. You gotta know how they use it, to use it to market to them!

Rating: 3 Stars | **Category:** resource

PINTEREST FOR BUSINESS NEWSLETTER - https://business.pinterest.com/en/contact-us

Love Pinterest? Want to love Pinterest? Want to learn to love Pinterest? They'll help you with their lively and self-promotional Pinterest for business newsletter. Get the inside scoop on Pinterest by Pinterest (for business users).

Rating: 3 Stars | **Category:** eletter

PINTEREST HELP TOPICS - https://help.pinterest.com/en/articles

Browse topic by topic through the Pinterest help pages. For example, learn the basics of what pins are and how to use them. Great for beginners.

Rating: 3 Stars | **Category:** resource

PINTEREST FOR BUSINESS - http://www.businessnewsdaily.com/7552-pinterest-business-guide.html

Pinterest can be used to promote your business, especially if you reach one of the two intertwined demographics: young women and shoppers. This brief but meaty article explains how.

Rating: 3 Stars | **Category:** archive

PINSTAMATIC - http://pinstamatic.com

This free tool can be used to quickly create visual content for Pinterest boards without any editing tools. Use it to add a website snapshot, quotes and text, sticky notes, Twitter profile, calendar date, location map, captioned photo, and even a Spotify track.

Rating: 3 Stars | **Category:** tool

PINTEREST FOR BUSINESS - https://business.pinterest.com

Looking to 'get started' on Pinterest? Here is the official site on how a business page for Pinterest works.

Rating: 3 Stars | **Category:** resource

ULTIMATE PINTEREST MARKETING GUIDE - https://blog.kissmetrics.com/ultimate-pinterest-marketing-guide/

> KISSmetrics has produced a landmark guide to how to use Pinterest for business. It's a great, basic read for the beginner.
>
> **Rating:** 3 Stars | **Category:** article

THE RETAILERS GUIDE TO PINTEREST - http://www.business2community.com/pinterest/retailers-guide-pinterest-01016672

> Business2community.com shares this short yet informative 'how to' article on what to do when, where, how, and why on Pinterest as a business.
>
> **Rating:** 3 Stars | **Category:** article

PINTEREST BUSINESS GUIDES - https://business.pinterest.com/en/pinterest-guides

> Downloadable business-friendly guides from Pinterest about how to use Pinterest effectively for your business.
>
> **Rating:** 3 Stars | **Category:** resource

VIRALWOOT - http://viralwoot.com

> This tool helps increase your Pinterest visibility by monitoring your Pinterest profile and pins. You can promote your pins and create pinalerts!
>
> **Rating:** 2 Stars | **Category:** tool

PINTEREST FACEBOOK PAGE TAB - http://woobox.com/pinterest

> This tool allows you to add a Pinterest tab to your Facebook page; another great way to integrate your social media marketing strategies! Get complete stats for page views, visits, and likes, segmented by fans and non-fans who view your Facebook page tab.
>
> **Rating:** 2 Stars | **Category:** tool

PINVOLVE - http://www.pinvolve.co/

This tool automatically syncs your Facebook and Pinterest pages, allowing you to integrate your social media marketing strategies. Free for one Facebook page with limited pinning.

Rating: 2 Stars | **Category:** tool

PINALERTS - http://pinalerts.com

Pinalerts allows you to receive email notifications whenever someone pins something from your website.

Rating: 2 Stars | **Category:** tool

PINTEREST BRAND GUIDELINES - https://business.pinterest.com/en/brand-guidelines

New to Pinterest? This set of guidelines will help any business use the Pinterest brand in their marketing. It includes information on the logo, badge, and what words or phrases are going to be most helpful and most appropriate for your marketing needs.

Rating: 2 Stars | **Category:** resource

TAILWIND - https://tailwindapp.com

This tool provides Pinterest analytics. Users can view total pins, repins, likes, followers and a graph of your score as well as schedule pins. Additionally, users can view influential followers.

Rating: 2 Stars | **Category:** tool

PIN SEARCH - https://chrome.google.com/webstore/detail/pin-search-image-search-o/okiaciimfpgbpdhnfdllhdkicpmdoakm

An extension for Chrome browser that allows users to easily find related photos and information for photos posted on Pinterest.

Rating: 2 Stars | **Category:** service

PINTEREST BLOG - https://business.pinterest.com/en/blog

The official blog by Pinterest about Pinterest, targeted at small businesses.

Rating: 2 Stars | **Category:** blog

7

INSTAGRAM

If a picture is worth a thousand words, is one Instagram follower worth a thousand Twitter followers? Who knows? Instagram (https://www.instagram.com/), owned by Facebook, is an up-and-coming social media.

Here are the best free tools and resources for Instagram marketing!

INSTAGRAM MARKETING GUIDE - http://socialmediaexaminer.com/instagram-marketing-guide

This guide from Social Media Examiner isn't (just) for Instagram newbies, as it includes links to SME articles on topics like integrating video and running contests. There's something for just about everyone here, from the marketing strategist to the social media practitioner. Check it and see.

Rating: 4 Stars | **Category:** resource

IconoSquare - http://iconosquare.com

This is a great, user-friendly tool to help you manage your business' Instagram account. The analytics section displays all the info you need about your posts: views, likes, comments and followers. Use this tool to manage your account and see which photos are getting traction.

Rating: 4 Stars | **Category:** tool

SnapWidget - http://snapwidget.com

Use this widget to quickly and easily embed an Instagram photos on your website or blog.

Rating: 4 Stars | **Category:** tool

INSTAGRAM FOR BUSINESS - https://business.instagram.com

Hey you're a business! Here's how to get on Instagram as a business, and use it to your advantage.

Rating: 4 Stars | **Category:** resource

IFTTT - https://ifttt.com

This app, If Then Then That, is a great tool for linking multiple social media accounts. It allows you to create 'recipes' that link your tools exactly the way you like them! For example: make a recipe that adds to a Google Apps spreadsheet every time a particular user uploads to Instagram - a great way to keep up with your competitors SMM strategies! With over 120 supported applications, the 'recipes' are endless, making this a good tool for your SMM strategies.

Rating: 4 Stars | **Category:** tool

TAG BOARD - https://tagboard.com/

Hashtags have moved beyond Twitter. This amazing cool tool allows you to take a hashtag and browse Facebook and Twitter and Instagram, etc., so see posts that relate to that hashtag. Then you can find related tags. Oh, and you can use it as a content discovery tool, too.

Rating: 4 Stars | **Category:** tool

SOCIALRANK - https://socialrank.com

If Instagram or Twitter are important to your business, you'll want to check out SocialRank. This tool provides analytics for both social networks (separately), in an easy to understand format. Instagram version isn't as multifaceted as the Twitter version, but both allow you to sort and filter your followers in many ways, including 'Most Valuable', 'Best Follower' and others. Note: this tool requires Instagram/Twitter authorization for use with these social networks.

Rating: 3 Stars | **Category:** tool

WEBSTA - http://websta.me

Websta is another Instagram web viewer, and provides functionality typical for this genre: browse, comment, & like posts, follow/unfollow users, see your followers/who you're following, organize posts into boards, share posts on social media, view statistics for your account, create an Instagram gallery for embedding on your blog or website, etc. Note: this tool requires Instagram authorization to use.

Rating: 3 Stars | **Category:** tool

TAGBOARD - http://tagboard.com

Hashtags started on Twitter, but now they are everywhere. Use this tool to research existing hashtags across a variety of social media, including Twitter, Facebook, Google+, Instagram, Flickr, Vine, and define your own. Fun and informative, too.

Rating: 3 Stars | **Category:** service

LATERGRAMME - https://www.latergram.me/

Hootsuite for Instagram: schedule posts into the future. In this way, you can make your Instagram account "look" like it's always active, but you can manage it on a scheduled basis. Go to the beach or go shopping.

Rating: 3 Stars | **Category:** service

SQUARELOVIN - https://squarelovin.com

Another great Instagram analytics tool. This tool shows you stats on your photo likes and comments as well as a daily track of followers gained and followers lost. A useful part of this tool is the the '10-most engaged followers' section - allowing you to see who your best customers might be! Use this tool to see what pictures are working for you and which ones aren't.

Rating: 3 Stars | **Category:** tool

INSTAGRAM FOR BUSINESS BLOG - http://blog.business.instagram.com

Here it is: the official blog by Instagram about Instagram, focused on how businesses can use Instagram to boost their social media presence..

Rating: 3 Stars | **Category:** blog

POSTRIS - http://postris.com/

An advanced, web-based Instagram dashboard for tracking and organizing your Instagram account and daily updates from leading publications and social networks. Helps users keep up with what is trending on Instagram

Rating: 3 Stars | **Category:** tool

GRAMFEED - http://gramfeed.com

Gramfeed allows users to search for Instagram posts based on location, both via hashtags and geotags (i.e., photos which have been geographically tagged with location data). It also allows keyword filtering on searches which, for example, would allow you to search for shoes in Los Angeles. Limited search results provided without Instagram login.

Rating: 3 Stars | **Category:** tool

GRAMBLR - http://gramblr.com

As a mobile app, Instagram forces users to take and upload photos via their mobile devices. Instead of jumping through hoops to get images from your computer (Mac/PC) onto Instagram, download and install Gramblr, free. Like all Instagram photos, your uploaded photos must be square (e.g., 640 px x 640 px), less than 500 KB, and Instagram filters aren't available, but a small price to pay.

Rating: 3 Stars | **Category:** tool

CROWDFIRE - http://crowdfireapp.com

Crowdfire is an interesting way to manage your relationships on both Instagram and Twitter (separately). With it, for example, you can manage fans (people who have followed you but whom you haven't followed), people who have recently unfollowed you, etc. Note: this tool requires Instagram/Twitter authorization for use with these social networks.

Rating: 3 Stars | **Category:** tool

COLLECTO - http://collec.to

Another great tool for checking your Instagram analytics. This tool gives you an overview of main engagement stats of your account as well as most liked, commented, and follower stats.

Rating: 3 Stars | **Category:** tool

INK361 - http://ink361.com

INK361 is a web viewer to view and manage your Instagram photos. Create albums, discover new contacts, sort who you follow into Circles, set up alerts for new posts. view statistics, see which filters are most popular, etc. Note: this tool requires Instagram authorization to use.

Rating: 2 Stars | **Category:** tool

FREE INSTAGRAM USER REPORT - http://simplymeasured.com/freebies/instagram-analytics

Social analytics tool company SimplyMeasured offers a 'free' report on any Instagram user but requires you to a) authenticate your Instagram account b) authorize sending a one-time tweet about the report via Twitter. If you can get past those hurdles, you will receive both a web-based and Excel version of the free report, which provides engagement metrics like total Instagram and Facebook Likes and comments. Engagement for specific images is available on a "Top Photos" spreadsheet, as are top comment keywords and best time or day for engagement.

Rating: 2 Stars | **Category:** tool

8

TWITTER

Do you Twitter? Do you know what a good Tweet is? What about a #hashtag? Or a retweet or a @handle? Twitter is a world unto itself, and some think it is the greatest time-waster since... blogging... or Facebook. But millions do Tweet and millions love Twitter (https://twitter.com/). For some businesses, Twitter can be an amazing marketing platform. For others, it's a huge waste of time.

Here are the best **free** tools and resources for Twitter marketing, ranked with the best first!

TWITTER ADVANCED SEARCH - https://twitter.com/search-advanced

Search to see what others are saying about topics relevant and your organization's interests, before, during, after you use Twitter. Here's a nifty trick: Use the 'Near this place' field to find people in a city near you tweeting on a topic like 'pizza.' Great for local brands.

Rating: 5 Stars | **Category:** tool

BUZZSUMO - http://buzzsumo.com/

Buzzsumo is a 'buzz' monitoring tool for social media. Input a website (domain) and/or a topic and see what people are sharing across Facebook, Twitter, Google+ and other social media. Great for link-building (because what people link to is what they share), and also for social media.

Rating: 5 Stars | **Category:** tool

HASHTAGIFY.ME - http://hashtagify.me

Hashtagify.me allows you to search tens of millions of Twitter hashtags and quickly find the best ones for your needs based on popularity, relationships, languages, influencers and other metrics. Also useful for SEO link building and keyword discovery.

Rating: 5 Stars | **Category:** tool

HASHTAGS.ORG - http://hashtags.org

Tool which attempts to organize the world's hashtags. Provides hashtag analytics for your brand, business, product, service, event or blog. Input words that matter to you, and Hashtags looks to see the trends on Twitter.

Rating: 4 Stars | **Category:** engine

TWITONOMY - http://twitonomy.com

Twitonomy is a free online Twitter analytics tool which provides a wealth of information about all aspects of Twitter, including in-depth stats on any Twitter user, insights on your followers, mentions, favorites & retweets, and analytics on hashtags. It also lets you monitor tweets, manage your lists, download tweets & reports, and much more. Definitely worth checking out if Twitter is part of your social media strategy.

Rating: 4 Stars | **Category:** tool

TWITAHOLIC - http://twitaholic.com

Tracks the most popular Twitter users based on followers. Use this to find top tweeters - sort of a top 100, 200, 300, etc list for the Twitterdom. Also just a great way to find out who's really famous on Twitter. Katy Perry, anyone?

Rating: 4 Stars | **Category:** service

SOCIALOOMPH - https://www.socialoomph.com/

SocialOomph is a powerful free (and paid) suite of tools to manage and schedule your Twitter and Facebook posts. Imagine going to the beach, forgetting about the office, yet having 67 different Tweets auto-posted...that's what SocialOomph is about. Use technology to appear busy and Facebooking / Tweeting all the time.

Rating: 4 Stars | **Category:** tool

SMALL BUSINESS GUIDE TO TWITTER - http://simplybusiness.co.uk/microsites/twitter-for-small-businesses

Interactive step-by-step flowchart to using Twitter for small business. Comprised of key questions and linked resources with more information. Covers everything from very basic to advanced topics.

Rating: 4 Stars | **Category:** resource

TWITTER ANALYTICS - https://analytics.twitter.com

The official page for Twitter analytics and metrics. Sign up via Twitter, and learn how your tweets are doing!

Rating: 4 Stars | **Category:** tool

BITLY - https://bitly.com

Bitly is a URL shortening service that will track your click-throughs. Very useful for email marketing, blogging, and Twitter.

Rating: 4 Stars | **Category:** service

TWITTER FOR BUSINESS - https://business.twitter.com

Straight from the bird's mouth...learn how to use Twitter for business.

Rating: 4 Stars | **Category:** overview

PAY WITH A TWEET - http://www.paywithatweet.com/

Viral / share promotion tool focusing on referral marketing. Entice users to 'pay with a Tweet' in order to receive a discount or some wonderful freebie. Includes a limited functionality, limited usage free plan.

Rating: 4 Stars | **Category:** tool

IFTTT - https://ifttt.com

This app, If Then Then That, is a great tool for linking multiple social media accounts. It allows you to create 'recipes' that link your tools exactly the way you like them! For example: make a recipe that adds to a Google Apps spreadsheet every time a particular user uploads to Instagram - a great way to keep up with your competitors SMM strategies! With over 120 supported applications, the 'recipes' are endless, making this a good tool for your SMM strategies.

Rating: 4 Stars | **Category:** tool

FOLLOWERWONK - https://moz.com/followerwonk/

Followerwonk helps you explore and grow your social graph. Dig deeper into Twitter analytics: Who are your followers? Where are they located? When do they tweet? Find and connect with new influencers in your niche. Use actionable visualizations to compare your social graph to others. Easily share your reports with the world. Brought to you by Moz.

Rating: 4 Stars | **Category:** tool

TWITTER HELP CENTER - https://support.twitter.com

Did you know Twitter has technical support? Yep, they do. It's relatively hidden, but here it is. It's more for users of Twitter, but it does have some juicy help for actual businesses on Twitter as well. Tweet, tweet, tweet.

Rating: 4 Stars | **Category:** resource

TAG BOARD - https://tagboard.com/

Hashtags have moved beyond Twitter. This amazing cool tool allows you to take a hashtag and browse Facebook and Twitter and Instagram, etc., so see posts that relate to that hashtag. Then you can find related tags. Oh, and you can use it as a content discovery tool, too.

Rating: 4 Stars | **Category:** tool

TAGDEF - https://tagdef.com

Looking to understand what a particular hashtag means? Use this nifty tool to define a hashtag and to research hashtags BEFORE you create or use them.

Rating: 4 Stars | **Category:** tool

TWEETDECK - https://tweetdeck.twitter.com

TweetDeck is your personal browser for staying in touch with what's happening now, connecting you with your contacts across Twitter, Facebook, MySpace, LinkedIn and more. Developed independently, now owned by Twitter.

Rating: 4 Stars | **Category:** service

KEYHOLE - http://keyhole.co

This tool provides real-time social conversation tracking for Twitter, Facebook, and Instagram. Use this tool to measure conversations around your business, identify prospective clients and influencers talking about your services, and find relevant content. Enables tracking of hashtags, keywords, and URLs.

Rating: 4 Stars | **Category:** tool

TWITTER COUNTER - http://twittercounter.com

Use this Twitter application to find out how many people follow you, growth, and other metrics.

Rating: 3 Stars | **Category:** service

CROWDFIRE - http://crowdfireapp.com

Crowdfire is an interesting way to manage your relationships on both Instagram and Twitter (separately). With it, for example, you can manage fans (people who have followed you but whom you haven't followed), people who have recently unfollowed you, etc. Note: this tool requires Instagram/Twitter authorization for use with these social networks.

Rating: 3 Stars | **Category:** tool

TAGBOARD - http://tagboard.com

Hashtags started on Twitter, but now they are everywhere. Use this tool to research existing hashtags across a variety of social media, including Twitter, Facebook, Google+, Instagram, Flickr, Vine, and define your own. Fun and informative, too.

Rating: 3 Stars | **Category:** service

TWIANGULATE - http://twiangulate.com

This nifty tool allows you to input up to three Twitter accounts. It then compares who follows each account and draws you a nifty map, plus identifies the most important followers, so you can see the 'network effect' of who follows whom on Twitter.

Rating: 3 Stars | **Category:** tool

ONALYTICA - http://content.onalytica.com/

Use your own content to find influencers on Twitter. Sound crazy? Well, basically nearly everything on Twitter sounds crazy. So this is less crazY: basically use keywords in your content marketing posts to identify potential folks who might actually share it on Twitter.

Rating: 3 Stars | **Category:** tool

TWITTER TOOLS - THE ULTIMATE LIST - http://twittertoolsbook.com/ultimate-list/

There are so many Twitter tools out there! This is the 'ultimate list' of Twitter tools, with a focus not just on marketing but all sorts of funny, zanny, and even useful tools for Twitter. Worth a read / glance / tweet.

Rating: 3 Stars | **Category:** article

WHAT THE TREND - http://whatthetrend.com

What the Trend tracks trends on Twitter. So it's what is going viral, now, on Twitter. Mainly mainstream media stuff.. but you can use their search feature to find trends that interest you. Brought to us by HootSuite.

Rating: 3 Stars | **Category:** service

LIKE EXPLORER - http://www.likeexplorer.com/

Type in a URL and see its shares across social media outlets, including Facebook, Twitter, Google+, LinkedIn, Pinterest, and StumbleUpon. Very useful for link-building and competitor research.

Rating: 3 Stars | **Category:** tool

TWEETJUKEBOX - http://www.tweetjukebox.com/

Tweet Jukebox will eliminate the need to continually schedule your tweets, and manage your content. It's all right at your fingertips. Once you turn on your jukebox, it tweets for you. Automatically. No more wasted time. How's that for good news?

Rating: 3 Stars | **Category:** tool

TWERIOD - http://www.tweriod.com/

Tweriod gives you the best times to tweet. It analyzes both your tweets and your followers' tweets, so you can start tweeting when it makes most sense to reach others.

Rating: 3 Stars | **Category:** tool

TWITTER BLOG - https://blog.twitter.com/

If Twitter is important to you, you should read this - the 'official' Twitter blog.

Rating: 3 Stars | **Category:** blog

CLICKTOTWEET - https://clicktotweet.com/

ClickToTweet is a great way to encourage social sharing, especially of blog posts. Nudge your users to tweet your content.

Rating: 3 Stars | **Category:** tool

SOCIALRANK - https://socialrank.com

If Instagram or Twitter are important to your business, you'll want to check out SocialRank. This tool provides analytics for both social networks (separately), in an easy to understand format. Instagram version isn't as multifaceted as the Twitter version, but both allow you to sort and filter your followers in many ways, including 'Most Valuable', 'Best Follower' and others. Note: this tool requires Instagram/Twitter authorization for use with these social networks.

Rating: 3 Stars | **Category:** tool

SUMALL - https://sumall.com

> This free tracking service will help you aggregate and monitor your key business and social media stats. With more than 30 platforms to choose from, SumAll is adaptable to your marketing needs.
>
> **Rating:** 3 Stars | **Category:** service

VINE - https://vine.co/

> Vine, owned by Twitter, is a video app / add-on. It shows VERY short videos that can be shared on Twitter.
>
> **Rating:** 3 Stars | **Category:** service

TWEET ARCHIVIST - http://www.tweetarchivist.com/

> Use this nifty service and tool to identify who is tweeting on your keywords and hashtags, and to analyze trends and data. In addition to Twitter, searches Instagram, Vine and Tumblr. Limited functionality for free, more with paid plans.
>
> **Rating:** 3 Stars | **Category:** tool

TWITTERFEED - http://twitterfeed.com

> Feed your blog to Twitter, Facebook, LinkedIn and other social networks, automagically.
>
> **Rating:** 2 Stars | **Category:** service

GOO.GL - GOOGLE URL SHORTENER - http://goo.gl

> Competitive with Bitly and Tinyurl comes Goo.gl - Google's official URL shortener.
>
> **Rating:** 2 Stars | **Category:** tool

9

YOUTUBE

Video is bigger than YouTube, especially now that Facebook has gone big into video. That said, YouTube still dominates the online video market almost as much as its parent, Google, dominates search. YouTube can be as simple as your company broadcasting interesting videos or as complicated as your own channel with interactive features for your fans. YouTube is social, YouTube is lively, and YouTube has a special relationship with Google. YouTube can go viral! Check out YouTube (https://www.youtube.com/), create a channel, upload some videos and join the video revolution!

Here are the best **free** tools and resources for marketing via YouTube, ranked with the best first!

YOUTUBE TOOLS - http://bitly.com/ytcreatecorner

YouTube has done more and more to make it easier to publish and promote videos. This page lists six tools: YouTube Capture, YouTube Editor, Captions, Audio Library, Slideshow and YouTube Analytics. All of them are fantastic, free tools about YouTube by YouTube.

Rating: 5 Stars | **Category:** resource

YOUTUBE CREATOR HUB - http://youtube.com/yt/creators

Help center for those creating YouTube content. Learn how to better edit your videos, get them up on YouTube, etc. Has lessons on growing your audience, boot camp, and how to get viewers and even how to earn money via YouTube.

Rating: 5 Stars | **Category:** resource

IMOVIE FOR MAC - https://apple.com/mac/imovie

Apple's free, downloadable movie / video editor. Great for making YouTube videos!

Rating: 4 Stars | **Category:** tool

YOUTUBE CAPTURE - https://youtube.com/capture

YouTube Capture is an app for your mobile phone, which makes it easy to capture and edit videos right on your phone. Imagine you are a marketer / retailer and you want to use your phone to easily capture customer interactions, and upload (quickly / easily) to YouTube. Get the picture?

Rating: 4 Stars | **Category:** tool

YOUTUBE ADVERTISING RESOURCES - https://www.youtube.com/yt/advertise/

YouTube wants you to advertise! But, it also hides some good free SEO-oriented resources here for how to use YouTube effectively. Worth a look, and a bookmark.

Rating: 4 Stars | **Category:** resource

YOUTUBE SPOTLIGHT - https://www.youtube.com/user/YouTube

Trying to understand YouTube? This is the official YouTube Channel by YouTube on YouTube. Use to to discover what's new and trending around the world from music to culture to Internet phenomena, must-watch videos from across YouTube, all in one place.

Rating: 4 Stars | **Category:** video

POPULAR ON YOUTUBE -
https://www.youtube.com/channel/UCF0pVplsI8R5kcAqgt0RqoA

An auto-generated collection of what's popular on YouTube, and - shall we say - 'going viral.' As a marketer, seek to observe and understand why things go viral and how to leverage the video popularity wave.

Rating: 4 Stars | **Category:** service

SMALL BUSINESS GUIDE TO YOUTUBE -
http://simplybusiness.co.uk/microsites/youtube-for-small-business

Interactive step-by-step flowchart to YouTube marketing. Comprised of key questions and linked resources with more information. Excellent resource. Worth a look.

Rating: 4 Stars | **Category:** resource

YOUTUBE HELP CENTER - http://support.google.com/youtube

The official help site for YouTube, conveniently located on Google. Google owns YouTube, but you already knew that.

Rating: 4 Stars | **Category:** overview

WINDOWS MOVIE MAKER - http://bitly.com/windowsmov

For those on the Windows platform, Movie Maker is the goto free program to edit videos for YouTube and other platforms.

Rating: 3 Stars | **Category:** tool

YouTube Creator Academy - http://creatoracademy.withgoogle.com

Learn tips and tricks from the YouTube pros to maximize your corporate YouTube page. Expert videos, tests, and even a way to 'meet' other YouTube content creators. Fun, friendly, and free.

Rating: 3 Stars | **Category:** resource

TubeChop - http://tubechop.com

Enter a YouTube video URL, watch it, and 'chop it' at the moment you want a user to see. This way, you can share just the portion of a video you want, rather than forcing people to watch a long boring intro or other non-relevant content.

Rating: 3 Stars | **Category:** tool

Wideo - http://wideo.co

An online video maker, similar to iMovie or Windows Movie Maker.

Rating: 3 Stars | **Category:** tool

YouTube Embed Tool (Customized) - http://www.classynemesis.com/projects/ytembed/

Sure you can embed YouTube videos directly, but this cool tool allows you to optimize and customize what you want to do. For example, start at a particular moment, or add easy social share buttons.

Rating: 3 Stars | **Category:** tool

YouTube Creator Studio Android App - http://bit.ly/1dqVLc2

Use YouTube Creator Studio to manage your channel from your Android phone. Great when you're on the go. For iTunes version go to http://bit.ly/yc-iphone.

Rating: 3 Stars | **Category:** tool

YOUTUBE BLOG - http://youtube-global.blogspot.com

The official YouTube blog. If YouTube is important to you - whether as a video hosting service and/or as a social media method to connect with customers - here is where you find the inside scoop on Google's YouTube service.

Rating: 3 Stars | **Category:** blog

YOUTUBE HELP CHANNEL - https://youtube.com/youtubehelp

More for general users than for marketers, the YouTube Help channel has informative videos on how to 'use' YouTube. That said, if you know how your customers use YouTube, you can become a better marketer towards them. Includes tutorials, troubleshooting, and tips. Never stop learning!

Rating: 3 Stars | **Category:** resource

YOUTUBE HELP FORUM - https://productforums.google.com/forum/#!forum/youtube

The new and improved forum by and about YouTube - user-generated content, helpful tips and pointers from official YouTubers. This is your 'goto' site if you want to post a question for the community and hopefully get some help.

Rating: 3 Stars | **Category:** resource

YOUTUBE ON FACEBOOK - https://www.facebook.com/youtube

Facebook is on YouTube, and so YouTube is on Facebook. Just 'Like" YouTube on Facebook and stay up-to-date with happenings on YouTube (on Faceboook). It's recursive!

Rating: 3 Stars | **Category:** resource

YOUTUBE EDITOR - https://www.youtube.com/editor

While there is Microsoft Windows Movie Maker and Apple iMovie, there is also a free YouTube editor for your videos. Not incredibly powerful, but free and easy to use 'in the cloud.'

Rating: 3 Stars | **Category:** tool

YOUTUBE ADVERTISERS CHANNEL - https://youtube.com/user/advertise

Interested in advertising on YouTube? This is the official channel with tons of useful, if salesy, content on why and how to advertise your products or services on YouTube. If you're into advertising, check out the 'Ads Leaderboard,' which highlights top ads month by month.

Rating: 3 Stars | **Category:** video

YOUTUBE CREATORS BLOG - http://youtubecreator.blogspot.com

The official YouTube blog by and about YouTube partners. You can pick up some good tips on YouTube marketing here, plus learn some ins and outs from YouTube superstars. Plus it's just plain fun to see what the YouTube famous are up to.

Rating: 3 Stars | **Category:** blog

REELSEO VIDEO MARKETER'S GUIDE - http://www.reelseo.com/

A leading resource for news, analysis, tips and trends for the online video and Internet marketing industries. Their videologists and columnists offer expert advice, guidance, and commentary about the world of online video to guide Internet marketers and video content producers on best practices and online video services that suit their needs.

Rating: 2 Stars | **Category:** portal

POWTOON - http://www.powtoon.com/

PowToon provides animated video production using the freemium pricing model. Play around with it to create animated videos to present anything you want about your business. Paid plans available, but you can do some cool stuff for free.

Rating: 2 Stars | **Category:** tool

YOUTUBE (BRAND) CHANNELS - https://support.google.com/youtube/topic/4601639

Brand channels on YouTube have an advertising component, but many of the items on this page are applicable to regular channels on YouTube as well. So this is a useful 'how to' article on managing a brand page on YouTube.

Rating: 2 Stars | **Category:** article

YOUTUBE ON TWITTER - https://twitter.com/youtube

YouTube's official Twitter profile (@YouTube). So does Twitter have an official channel on YouTube? This could get weird.

Rating: 2 Stars | **Category:** resource

YOUTUBE ON GOOGLE+ - https://plus.google.com/+youtube

If you are really into YouTube, follow them on social media. Here is their Google+ page.

Rating: 1 Stars | **Category:** resource

10

LOCAL

Local search is people looking for restaurants, bars, clubs, etc. But local search is also people looking for hair stylists, plumbers, attorneys, or hypnotherapists. Many businesses have a local aspect, and many customers begin their search for local at Google.com. Others start at Yelp, Citysearch.com, or Judy's Books. Whether it's Google My Business (https://www.google.com/business), Yelp (http://www.yelp.com) or another service – you can (and should) pay attention!

Local is important for both SEO and SMM. Here are the best **free** tools and resources for local search / social media marketing, ranked with the best first!

GOOGLE MY BUSINESS (GOOGLE LOCAL / GOOGLE PLACES) -
https://business.google.com/

> Google My Business is the new official name, but behind-the-scenes they still call it Google Places or Google Local or Google+ Local. Or whatchamacallit. This is the official entry point to find and claim your small business listing on Google's local service.
>
> **Rating:** 5 Stars | **Category:** resource

GOOGLE+ REVIEW LINK GENERATOR - https://www.grade.us/home/labs/google-review-link-generator

> Lost as to how to find your company's Google+ reviews? Use this nifty tool to find the exact URL for your reviews. You can also use this to give to clients, directly.
>
> **Rating:** 5 Stars | **Category:** tool

YELP - http://biz.yelp.com

> Yelp is a local reviews service. Businesses can have (and claim) a FREE listing on Yelp, which can be helpful for local listings and local link building. This link is to the 'business' portal at Yelp - how to find, and list your business.
>
> **Rating:** 5 Stars | **Category:** service

BING PLACES FOR BUSINESS (BING LOCAL) - https://www.bingplaces.com/

> Bing is a distant #2 to Google, behind probably Yahoo...but nonetheless, for local search purposes, it's still valuable to find (and claim) your local listing on Bing Local. So go for it, be a Binger!
>
> **Rating:** 5 Stars | **Category:** service

GOOGLE MY BUSINESS (GOOGLE+ LOCAL / GOOGLE PLACES) HELP CENTER -
https://support.google.com/business#topic=4539639

> A wonderful and rather hidden microsite in the Googleplex with many help topics to learn about, modify, and update your Google+ Local listings. Google Local

begot Google Places begot Google+ Local begot Google My Business. You and I both wish Google would settle on a name for its local service!

Rating: 5 Stars | **Category:** resource

MOZ LOCAL - https://moz.com/local

If local matters to you, you need to see where you're listed (Google+, Yelp, etc.), and how you're listed. You also want consistent address, phone number, and other data across local sites (called 'citations'). Moz has a new paid service for this, but this free tool will analyze (and find) your listings pretty easily.

Rating: 5 Stars | **Category:** tool

GOOGLE+ PAGE SEARCH - http://www.gpluspagesearch.com/

Use this nifty site to find competitor Google+ pages easily. Just enter a competitor name (or your own business name), and this search engine will identify the relevant Google+ page.

Rating: 5 Stars | **Category:** tool

REVIEWBUZZ - http://www.reviewbuzz.com/

This is the new (PAID) thing in local review marketing. Services like this, ask customers to first rate you, and then if, and ONLY IF, they like you, the customer is prompted to leave a review on Google / Yelp, etc. Probably a violation of the official terms of service, but this is probably the future of the thin gray line between what's allowed and what's not. USE AT YOUR OWN RISK.

Rating: 4 Stars | **Category:** service

SMALL BUSINESS GUIDE TO GOOGLE MY BUSINESS -
http://www.simplybusiness.co.uk/microsites/google-my-business-guide/

Interactive step-by-step flowchart to using Google My Business. Comprised of key questions and linked resources with more information. Chart is divided into different areas including setup, page management and optimization, engagement and reviews, and citations.

Rating: 4 Stars | **Category:** resource

YELP HELP CENTER - http://www.yelp-support.com/

Here is the official Yelp help center, for both consumer and businesses. If you are new to local marketing, this is a great place to understand how it works from an official Yelp perspective. Remember, however, that what is officially presented as 'how Yelp works' isn't 100% accurate.

Rating: 4 Stars | **Category:** resource

YELP SUPPORT CENTER (FOR BUSINESS OWNERS) - http://www.yelp-support.com/Yelp_for_Business_Owners?l=en_US

Yelp's site to support both users and businesses. As a business owner, click on the links to the left, or on 'Yelp for Business Owners' card. It's better than nothing, but Yelp still has a long way to go to be easy-to-use for business owners. Easy password reset?

Rating: 4 Stars | **Category:** resource

YEXT - http://www.yext.com/

Follow the instructions to 'scan your business.' This nifty tool allows you to input your business name and phone number and it will go out and find all the relevant listings across many, many different local listings services. Then you can (pay) to have it fix many of them. Not perfect, but a good start on identifying logical local listing opportunities for your business.

Rating: 4 Stars | **Category:** tool

GOOGLE PLACES CATEGORIES - http://blumenthals.com/google-lbc-categories/

When setting up your free listing on Google Places, be sure to choose categories that are already existing. Use this to tool help you identify extant categories as you work on your five free categories for Google Places. Perform a search by entering a term or click the search button.

Rating: 4 Stars | **Category:** tool

CITATION BUILDING STRATEGIES - THE COMPLETE LIST FOR LOCAL BUSINESSES - http://www.localstampede.com/citation-building-strategies-list/

It's always great when someone has done the brainstorming for you. If you are a local business, local 'citations' or links are incredibly helpful.

Rating: 4 Stars | **Category:** article

BEST LOCAL CITATIONS BY CATEGORY - https://moz.com/learn/local/citations-by-category

If you're 'into local,' then you gotta know your citation sources. Obviously, Google+ is the most important for Google, and in many markets Yelp is #2. But for a plumber vs. a chiropractor, where to get citations (listings on local sites) can be different. Moz breaks out the 'best' citation sources by common category.

Rating: 4 Stars | **Category:** article

LOCAL RANK CHECKING VIA ADWORDS - https://adwords.google.com/apt/AdPreview

This is the OFFICIAL Google AdWords preview tool. But, guess what. You can use this to vary your city location, and check your rank against various cities. If, for example, you are a pizza restaurant serving San Jose, Milpitas, and Santa Clara, you can type in 'Pizza' and see your rank in different cities. You can login to your AdWord account and click Tools - Preview Tool or use this direct link.

Rating: 4 Stars | **Category:** tool

GOOGLE MY BUSINESS (GOOGLE PLACES / GOOGLE LOCAL) HELP CENTER - https://support.google.com/business

Help with Google Places, conveniently hidden by Google..but here is where you can browse helpful articles on setting up and managing your free advertising and promotion efforts via Google Places.

Rating: 4 Stars | **Category:** resource

GOOGLE AND YOUR BUSINESS HELP FORUM -

https://www.en.advertisercommunity.com/t5/Google-My-Business/ct-p/GMB#

Forums by people using Google Places, er Google and Your Business. You can get help from the community here, which is often more effective than those annoying canned emails you get from Google itself!

Rating: 4 Stars | **Category:** resource

GET FIVE STARS - https://www.getfivestars.com/

This is the new (PAID) thing in local review marketing. Services like this, ask customers to first rate you, and then if, and ONLY IF, they like you, the customer is prompted to leave a review on Google / Yelp, etc. Probably a violation of the official terms of service, but this is probably the future of the thin gray line between what's allowed and what's not. USE AT YOUR OWN RISK.

Rating: 4 Stars | **Category:** service

SEO LOCAL RANKING FACTORS 2015 - https://moz.com/blog/local-search-ranking-factors-2015

Moz.com does a great job of first surveying SEO's and then compiling its best guestimate on the factors (in order) that propel a company to the top of local searches on Google.

Rating: 4 Stars | **Category:** resource

BRIGHTLOCAL REVIEWBIZ WIDGET - http://brightlocal.com/seo-tools/review-biz

Technically not a free tool, but getting reviews is so important, and this little widget makes an all-in-one how to ask for a review widget.

Rating: 3 Stars | **Category:** tool

LOCAL KEYWORD LIST GENERATOR - http://5minutesite.com/local_keywords.php

Don't know your local geography? What about all those pesky zip codes and small suburban towns? Enter a zip code or city into this tool, and it generates a nifty list of possible nearby locales and zips for your SEO efforts. A time saver if local search is important to your SEO.

Rating: 3 Stars | **Category:** tool

YELP BLOG FOR BUSINESS OWNERS - https://biz.yelp.com/blog

If local SEO / local SMM / Yelp matters to you, well, you MUST subscribe to and follow the official Yelp blog. Take it all with a grain of salt and a good dose of skepticism, as it is the OFFICIAL blog, so it gives you a good dose of Yelp-is-so-fantastic propaganda, but it is the official source.

Rating: 3 Stars | **Category:** blog

GOOGLE REVIEW HANDOUT GENERATOR - https://www.whitespark.ca/review-handout-generator

This very slick tool allows you to input your company, website, and logo and then it generates a very nice-looking PDF / handout you can give your clients and thereby solicit Google reviews. The PDF is very well done.

Rating: 3 Stars | **Category:** tool

GEORANKER - https://www.georanker.com/register

With both a free and paid version, this tool checks your company's rank on Google based on DIFFERENT locations. Useful if you have multiple locations, or want to rank in different communities, and you want accurate data.

Rating: 3 Stars | **Category:** service

YELP WEBINARS FOR BUSINESS - https://biz.yelp.com/blog/upcoming-webinar-schedule-2

Yelp produces OFFICIAL webinars not only on Yelp advertising but on how to create a good free listing. All of this with the caveat that they only tell you the official stuff, not the secret tips and tricks, but still worth while.

Rating: 1 Stars | **Category:** blog

11

EMAIL

Email marketing is the *Rodney Dangerfield* of social media marketing: *it don't get no respect*. Yet it's incredibly important. "Liking" a company on Facebook, after all, is a lot less intrusive than giving them permission to send you personalized emails. Our email inboxes are the holy grail of all marketers!

In that spirit, here are the best free tools and resources for email marketing!

EMAIL MARKETING WIKIPEDIA ENTRY - http://en.wikipedia.org/wiki/E-mail_marketing

> Wikipedia, the free encyclopedia, provides a decent introduction to the subject of email marketing including details about spam laws in the US, Canada, and Europe.

> **Rating:** 5 Stars | **Category:** overview

HTML TO TEXT EMAIL CONVERTER - http://templates.mailchimp.com/resources/html-to-text

> Since some of your email newsletter subscribers prefer text vs HTML-based email messages, it's important to send both HTML and text versions of your mass email messages so their email client can display the format they prefer. Use this handy tool to quickly convert your HTML email newsletter into a format your text-based email subscribers will appreciate.

> **Rating:** 4 Stars | **Category:** tool

UNTORCH - https://untorch.com

> This is an email / viral promotion tool. You establish a 'freebie,' and then this tool gives you code that requires users to 'share' your freebie to get it. Service is not free and charges by the campaign per year.

> **Rating:** 4 Stars | **Category:** tool

GOOGLE ANALYTICS CAMPAIGNS URL BUILDER - https://support.google.com/analytics/answer/1033867

> Use this tool to build URLs to track your ad campaigns. For instance, if you have ad campaigns on Facebook or LinkedIn, or an email newsletter, you can use this tool from Google to make them easier to track in Google Analytics.

> **Rating:** 4 Stars | **Category:** tool

SMALL BUSINESS GUIDE TO EMAIL MARKETING - http://www.simplybusiness.co.uk/microsites/email-marketing-guide/

Interactive step-by-step flowchart to email marketing. Comprised of key questions and linked resources from around the web with more information. Thorough and well-done.

Rating: 4 Stars | **Category:** resource

THE HEMINGWAY APP - http://www.hemingwayapp.com/

Let's face it. Americans, and people everywhere, aren't getting smarter. This app allows you to paste in text from your blog post or email, and check the 'grade level.' It also identifies hard-to-read sentences. Can you say DUM IT DOWNE?

Rating: 4 Stars | **Category:** tool

ASCEND DIGITAL MARKETING SUMMIT - http://www.ascendsummit.com/

Sponsored by AWeber, the email marketing firm, this conference is actually more than just email marketing. It's about email marketing, about social, and about content. Plus some tools, and plus some experts (and of course pseudo-experts, what social media conference would be an SMM conference without hype?).

Rating: 4 Stars | **Category:** conference

CSS INLINER TOOL - http://templates.mailchimp.com/resources/inline-css

Since some email services and email clients strip out important elements like <head> and <style> from HTML email messages, it's important the styles in your email messages appear inline within your markup. Use this handy tool from MailChimp to convert your HTML email messages to a more email friendly format.

Rating: 4 Stars | **Category:** tool

EMAIL SPAM CHECKER - http://info.contactology.com/check-mqs

Another tool to check the deliverability of your (mass) email messages before sending, this one from Contactology. This one provides a useful HTML option, and assigns a score which assesses not only message deliverability but also the likelihood it will display correctly across all email readers (including webmail such as Gmail and Yahoo).

Rating: 4 Stars | **Category:** tool

EMAIL PREVIEW TOOL - http://info.contactology.com/email-view

Despite the ubiquity of HTML, neither web browsers nor email clients or email services render HTML-based email messages the same way. After you've created your HTML-based newsletter or other communication, paste it into this tool to see how it will display in web-based email services like Gmail, Hotmail, AOL, Yahoo and email clients like Outlook and Thunderbird.

Rating: 4 Stars | **Category:** tool

CONSTANT CONTACT - http://constantcontact.com

Constant Contact is an online marketing company that enables users create and manage email marketing campaigns like email newsletters, online surveys, event invitations, and promotions, and their email lists to more effectively connect with customers.

Rating: 3 Stars | **Category:** service

CAN-SPAM ACT OF 2003 WIKIPEDIA ENTRY - http://en.wikipedia.org/wiki/CAN-SPAM_Act_of_2003

Wikipedia, the free encyclopedia, provides an overview of the CAN-SPAM (Controlling the Assault of Non-Solicited Pornography And Marketing) Act of 2003. Important information all email marketers must understand and live by.

Rating: 3 Stars | **Category:** overview

MAILCHIMP - http://mailchimp.com

MailChimp is a web-based email marketing service. It helps you design email newsletters, share them on social networks, integrate with services, and track your results.

Rating: 3 Stars | **Category:** service

EMAIL BLACKLIST CHECK - http://mxtoolbox.com/blacklists.aspx

The IP address of the email server from where email messages are sent is important in determining if they ultimately arrive at their destination. IP addresses of email servers used to send spam are blacklisted, preventing other, legitimate messages sent from the same IP address (but different domains) from successful delivery. If you suspect your email messages aren't reaching their intended recipients, enter the IP address of your email server in this handy tool to check it against over 100 DNS based email blacklists.

Rating: 3 Stars | **Category:** tool

OPT-IN EMAIL MARKETING 101 - http://charlwood.com/opt-in_email_marketing.html

This article describes a detailed 10 step process when creating an opt-in email marketing campaigns created by Charlwood eMarketing, a registered B2B email list broker and online direct marketing agency. The agency is experienced in B2B cost per lead generation and provides opt-in email list services.

Rating: 3 Stars | **Category:** overview

EMAIL DESIGN REFERENCE - http://templates.mailchimp.com/

If the mechanics of sending HTML-based email messages to subscribers is a mystery, this guide provides an excellent primer. It describes basic concepts, designing, developing and testing mass HTML email messages, all important to making sure your email not only reaches its destination, but looks good when it arrives.

Rating: 3 Stars | **Category:** resource

AWEBER - https://www.aweber.com/

AWeber, along with Constant Contact, is one of more established email service providers, though they don't offer a free plan. Pricing starts at $19/month, with first month free/30-day free trial.

Rating: 3 Stars | **Category:** service

NEW EMAIL TEST - https://putsmail.com/tests/new

Want to see what a proposed email message will look like in your inbox? Use this nifty, free tool to test your email messages. Testing is the key to successful email campaigns.

Rating: 3 Stars | **Category:** tool

PREMAILER - http://premailer.dialect.ca/

Pre-flight for HTML email. Meaning, take an existing HTML document and this tool converts it to in-line HTML CSS. This is useful for emails as you need (should) use in-line CSS.

Rating: 3 Stars | **Category:** tool

12
BOOKMARKING

What could be more private than your Web bookmarks? How quaint! Bookmarking has gone social at sites such as Delicious (http://www.delicious.com/), StumbleUpon (http://www.stumbleupon.com/), Digg (http://www.digg.com/) and Reddit (http://www.reddit.com/).

Here are the best **free** resources on Social Bookmarking, ranked with the best first!

DELICIOUS.COM - https://delicious.com/

Social bookmarking site, now owned by Yahoo. Find pages others have bookmarked using keywords.

Rating: 5 Stars | **Category:** service

GOOGLE BOOKMARKS - http://google.com/bookmarks

Google's entry into the crowded and not so popular (but SEO-friendly) arena of social bookmarking.

Rating: 5 Stars | **Category:** service

PINTEREST - https://www.pinterest.com/

Pinterest is a social network in its own right, highly focused on visual search and shopping. Very, very big among shoppers like wedding brides and grooms, cooks and chefs, and anything visual (think interior design). It also functions as a social bookmarking site.

Rating: 4 Stars | **Category:** service

ADDTHIS - http://www.addthis.com/

Increase your traffic and page rank with the #1 bookmarking and sharing service, served over 20 billion times per month. This free service allows you to help people to use social media to link to or publicize your website. One click (well two clicks) and they can Tweet you, Facebook you, Email you or whatever their little social media heart desires.

Rating: 4 Stars | **Category:** service

REDDIT - https://www.reddit.com/

Reddit, which calls itself 'the front page of the Internet', is a popular site for social news browsing. The site has useful tabs such as 'new', 'rising', and 'controversial' that you can use for your viral marketing needs. Users can upvote or downvote articles giving you another heuristic to gauge what's trending now. The most upvoted stories can reach Reddit's front page. Reddit organizes topics by subreddits (i.e., forums). Despite its spartan user interface, it is used by many in the tech community to share favorite news stories.

Rating: 3 Stars | **Category:** portal

STUMBLEUPON - http://www.stumbleupon.com/

StumbleUpon is an online social bookmarking network which allows users to discover, rate, and share interesting web pages, photos and videos using peer-sourcing and social-networking principles. Use it to add your website pages and drive traffic to your site.

Rating: 3 Stars | **Category:** engine

DIGG - http://digg.com/

Digg is really a social news meets social bookmarking site. Diggers 'digg' stories they find compelling, and others can follow what is being 'digged' or 'dugg.'

Rating: 3 Stars | **Category:** portal

HUBPAGES - http://hubpages.com/

HubPages is an open community of passionate people—writers, explorers, knowledge seekers, conversation starters. Interacting and informing. Sharing words, pictures and videos. Asking questions. Finding answers. It's a rich and rewarding experience with a unique set of tools and resources to help Hubbers find and build an audience, easily create articles, and earn all sorts of rewards, from accolades to ad revenue. Over 27 million people explore HubPages every month.

Rating: 2 Stars | **Category:** engine

13

VIRAL MARKETING

Viruses can travel from person to person in the real world. So too in the Social Media world, a video, a post, a widget, a comment - almost anything can 'go viral.' Indeed the very *social* nature of Social Media makes it ideal for viral marketing - whether good or bad.

Here are the best **free** tools and resources on viral marketing, ranked with the best first!

BUZZFEED - http://www.buzzfeed.com/trending

What is going viral on the Web right now? Buzzfeed is a service that tracks virality. What is going viral - who would know? One of the cooler things it offers is users who 'predict' what will go viral, including the ability to follow the ones with better predictive records. So now viral has its own predictors.

Rating: 5 Stars | **Category:** portal

WHAT'S TRENDING - http://whatstrending.com

Ever wonder what's trending? This site can answer exactly that question! This site features the most popular videos and latest trends keeping users in the know. A useful heuristic is the color-coded views icon, which tells you how many people have viewed the post, making it easy to find the most popular posts. Content ranges from 'Man wears beard of bees' to international news.

Rating: 4 Stars | **Category:** portal

UNTORCH - https://untorch.com

This is an email / viral promotion tool. You establish a 'freebie,' and then this tool gives you code that requires users to 'share' your freebie to get it. Service is not free and charges by the campaign per year.

Rating: 4 Stars | **Category:** tool

PAY WITH A TWEET - http://www.paywithatweet.com/

Viral / share promotion tool focusing on referral marketing. Entice users to 'pay with a Tweet' in order to receive a discount or some wonderful freebie. Includes a limited functionality, limited usage free plan.

Rating: 4 Stars | **Category:** tool

POPULAR ON YOUTUBE - https://www.youtube.com/channel/UCF0pVplsI8R5kcAqgtoRq0A

An auto-generated collection of what's popular on YouTube, and - shall we say - 'going viral.' As a marketer, seek to observe and understand why things go viral and how to leverage the video popularity wave.

Rating: 4 Stars | **Category:** service

DIGG - http://digg.com/

Digg is really a social news meets social bookmarking site. Diggers 'digg' stories they find compelling, and others can follow what is being 'digged' or 'dugg.'

Rating: 3 Stars | **Category:** portal

POPURLS - http://popurls.com

See what's trending everywhere. Popurls is a news aggregator which lists popular stories being shared by major web sources and by category (including technology, politics, business, entertainment, sports, etc.) making it a window into viral marketing everywhere.

Rating: 3 Stars | **Category:** service

SNIP.LY - http://snip.ly

Share other people's content, but add your own image or text link to promote yourself. So in a sense you can 'hijack' some content from others to promote your own stuff (cue Dr. Evil laugh).

Rating: 3 Stars | **Category:** tool

TREND HUNTER BUSINESS - http://trendhunter.com/business

If you need some blog post creation inspiration, check out Trend Hunter Business, part of the larger Trend Hunter network of sites covering trends in everything from technology, lifestyle, culture, design, and 'bizarre'. With its handy filtering tools at the top of the page and infinite scrolling, you'll find something to spur your imagination in no time.

Rating: 3 Stars | **Category:** resource

WHAT THE TREND - http://whatthetrend.com

What the Trend tracks trends on Twitter. So it's what is going viral, now, on Twitter. Mainly mainstream media stuff.. but you can use their search feature to find trends that interest you. Brought to us by HootSuite.

Rating: 3 Stars | **Category:** service

REDDIT - https://www.reddit.com/

Reddit, which calls itself 'the front page of the Internet', is a popular site for social news browsing. The site has useful tabs such as 'new', 'rising', and 'controversial' that you can use for your viral marketing needs. Users can upvote or downvote articles giving you another heuristic to gauge what's trending now. The most upvoted stories can reach Reddit's front page. Reddit organizes topics by subreddits (i.e., forums). Despite its spartan user interface, it is used by many in the tech community to share favorite news stories.

Rating: 3 Stars | **Category:** portal

THE VERGE - http://theverge.com

The Verge is a site that posts articles about what's happening now, ranging from trending celebrities to the latest tech craze. The site has useful features such as the 'Trending Now' tab at the top and the 'TL;DR' section when you need news fast. It also features videos and forums.

Rating: 3 Stars | **Category:** portal

ALLTOP - http://alltop.com

Alltop, founded by Guy Kawasaki, is a new way to search for topics. Choose a topic and search to find the hottest, most popular, newest buzz going on that topic. Great way to find out not what something is, but what is happening in that topic area.

Rating: 2 Stars | **Category:** service

NEWSVINE - http://newsvine.com

Newsvine is a community journalism site where users post external links to articles they're currently reading. Users can comment and vote on the content, giving more information on what's trending now. Another useful feature of the site is the 'Recently Popular Discussions' section that shows which articles are going viral now.

Rating: 2 Stars | **Category:** portal

I WASTE SO MUCH TIME - http://iwastesomuchtime.com

Unlike most visitors of this site, you can use this tool productively for all your viral marketing needs! Find out what memes, tweets, and Tumblr posts are popular on the web now. This site also features 'top videos' and 'top images'. Sort by day, week, month, or all time to find what's trending now and what's on the rise.

Rating: 2 Stars | **Category:** portal

LIST OF INTERNET PHENOMENA WIKIPEDIA ENTRY -
http://en.wikipedia.org/wiki/List_of_Internet_phenomena

From a marketer's perspective, this Wikipedia article should be named What Goes Viral (And Why). Read this list, carefully, and look for the patterns of what goes viral and why, as well as what went viral when. It's a fascinating timeline and look at the age of viral marketing, Internet-style.

Rating: 2 Stars | **Category:** article

GOOGLE TRENDS - https://www.google.com/trends/

Use Google's interface to monitor keyword trends! This tool is like the person in High School voted 'most likely to succeed' and then he totally failed, and now is either in jail, homeless or dead. Google has ALL the cool trending information on search, and yet they produce this pathetic, useless, teasy-tease tool. Oh Google - you are such a tease!

Rating: 1 Stars | **Category:** tool

14
TOOLS

Surprisingly, there are not that many, general, all-purpose, free tools for understanding and deploying Social Media - at least not yet. Most are for cross-posting to Facebook, Twitter, MySpace, and LinkedIn. A few help you monitor or figure out what's going on in the conversation space. Still others help you encourage social use of your website or other social media venues.

Here are the best **free** Social Media Tools (of a general variety), ranked with the best first!

HOOTSUITE - https://hootsuite.com/

Manage all of your social media accounts, including multiple Twitter profiles through HootSuite. HootSuite makes it easy to manage multiple users over various social media accounts and allows you to track statistics. LOVE THIS TOOL!

Rating: 5 Stars | **Category:** vendor

BUZZSUMO - http://buzzsumo.com/

Buzzsumo is a 'buzz' monitoring tool for social media. Input a website (domain) and/or a topic and see what people are sharing across Facebook, Twitter, Google+ and other social media. Great for link-building (because what people link to is what they share), and also for social media.

Rating: 5 Stars | **Category:** tool

SOCIALOOMPH - https://www.socialoomph.com/

SocialOomph is a powerful free (and paid) suite of tools to manage and schedule your Twitter and Facebook posts. Imagine going to the beach, forgetting about the office, yet having 67 different Tweets auto-posted...that's what SocialOomph is about. Use technology to appear busy and Facebooking / Tweeting all the time.

Rating: 4 Stars | **Category:** tool

IFTTT - https://ifttt.com

This app, If Then Then That, is a great tool for linking multiple social media accounts. It allows you to create 'recipes' that link your tools exactly the way you like them! For example: make a recipe that adds to a Google Apps spreadsheet every time a particular user uploads to Instagram - a great way to keep up with your competitors SMM strategies! With over 120 supported applications, the 'recipes' are endless, making this a good tool for your SMM strategies.

Rating: 4 Stars | **Category:** tool

BUFFER - https://buffer.com/

Schedule tweets and other social media activity in the future. Competitor to Hootsuite.

Rating: 4 Stars | **Category:** tool

BITLY - https://bitly.com

Bitly is a URL shortening service that will track your click-throughs. Very useful for email marketing, blogging, and Twitter.

Rating: 4 Stars | **Category:** service

SHORTSTACK - http://www.shortstack.com/

ShortStack is a nifty program to optimize your social media campaigns on platforms like Facebook, Twitter, Instagram and Pinterest. On Facebook, ShortStack provides polls and surveys, contents, and forms for newsletter signups, contact us, etc. and is free for Business Pages up to a certain number of Likes. No expiring trials. No credit card required.

Rating: 4 Stars | **Category:** service

SHARETHIS - http://www.sharethis.com/get-sharing-tools/

Use this widget on your website to allow users to easily share your content. Competitive to Addthis.com.

Rating: 4 Stars | **Category:** tool

KNOWEM SOCIAL MEDIA OPTIMIZER - http://smo.knowem.com

This tool analyzes a Web URL, such as a blog post or your home page, to verify you are using the MICRODATA formats to communicate with Google and other social media sites. Does not always report accurate data, however.

Rating: 3 Stars | **Category:** tool

KNOWEM - http://knowem.com

Use KnowEm to check the availability of your business name across social networks like Facebook, Twitter, LinkedIn, etc. An all-in-one shop for researching potential brand identity across social media.

Rating: 3 Stars | **Category:** tool

ZAPIER - https://zapier.com

This tool allows users to not only see analytics but to create 'zaps'- instructions to combine your tools exactly how you like them! For example, create a 'zap' that adds to a Google Apps spreadsheet every time you receive a new Twitter follower. With hundreds of combinations this tool is easily adaptable for all you SMM needs. Competitor to IFTTT.

Rating: 2 Stars | **Category:** tool

TWITTERFEED - http://twitterfeed.com

Feed your blog to Twitter, Facebook, LinkedIn and other social networks, automagically.

Rating: 2 Stars | **Category:** service

GOO.GL - GOOGLE URL SHORTENER - http://goo.gl

Competitive with Bitly and Tinyurl comes Goo.gl - Google's official URL shortener.

Rating: 2 Stars | **Category:** tool

15

MONITORING

Sometimes we do not want to talk... We want to listen. Or measure. Social Media can be an amazing way to learn from customers - their comments, their reviews, their criticisms, and even their complaints. There are few free tools for monitoring and measuring, but we identify those that we know. For larger companies there are paid services that help monitor the social conversation.

Here are the best **free** resources on Social Media monitoring and metrics, ranked with the best first!

SOCIAL MENTION - http://socialmention.com

Social Mention is a social media search and analysis platform that aggregates user generated content from across the universe into a single stream of information. Use it to search Twitter, Facebook, and other social media sites for mentions in addition to other useful information like keywords used to search for topics entered.

Rating: 5 Stars | **Category:** engine

FEEDLY - http://feedly.com/

Feedly is a newsreader integrated with Google+ or Facebook. It's useful for social media because you can follow important blogs or other content and share it with your followers. It can also spur great blog ideas.

Rating: 5 Stars | **Category:** resource

BUZZSUMO - http://buzzsumo.com/

Buzzsumo is a 'buzz' monitoring tool for social media. Input a website (domain) and/or a topic and see what people are sharing across Facebook, Twitter, Google+ and other social media. Great for link-building (because what people link to is what they share), and also for social media.

Rating: 5 Stars | **Category:** tool

GOOGLE EMAIL ALERTS - https://www.google.com/alerts

Use Google to alert you by email for search results that matter to you. Input your company name, for example, to see when new web pages, blog posts, or other items surface on the web. Enter your target keywords to keep an eye on yourself and your competitors. Part of the Gmail system.

Rating: 4 Stars | **Category:** service

GOOGLE NEWS - https://news.google.com/

Excellent for reputation management as well as keeping up-to-date on specific keywords that matter to you and your business. First, sign in to your Google account or gmail. Second, customize Google news for your interest. Third, monitor your reputation as well as topics that matter to you. Go Google!

Rating: 4 Stars | **Category:** service

KEYHOLE - http://keyhole.co

This tool provides real-time social conversation tracking for Twitter, Facebook, and Instagram. Use this tool to measure conversations around your business, identify prospective clients and influencers talking about your services, and find relevant content. Enables tracking of hashtags, keywords, and URLs.

Rating: 4 Stars | **Category:** tool

TAGBOARD - https://tagboard.com

Tagboard uses the hashtag to aggregate content from multiple social media networks (e.g., Twitter, Facebook, Instagram), displaying it in a comprehensive and engaging visual format.

Rating: 3 Stars | **Category:** resource

SUMALL - https://sumall.com

This free tracking service will help you aggregate and monitor your key business and social media stats. With more than 30 platforms to choose from, SumAll is adaptable to your marketing needs.

Rating: 3 Stars | **Category:** service

MENTION - https://mention.com/en/

Similar to Google Alerts. Enter your email address and get free email alerts when topics are mentioned. For example, use your company name (personal name) and monitor your reputation online.

Rating: 3 Stars | **Category:** service

WHAT DO YOU LOVE? - http://www.wdyl.com/

Despite its name, What do you love? is really an interesting monitoring service by Google. Type in a keyword that you want to 'monitor' and Google will build out all sorts of searches and monitoring tools. It's very cool, but we're not completely sure why it's called "What do you love?"

Rating: 3 Stars | **Category:** tool

NUTSHELLMAIL - http://nutshellmail.com

An email tool for monitoring social media. NutshellMail tracks your brand's social media activity and delivers a summary to your email inbox on your schedule. Brought to us by email marketing company ConstantContact.

Rating: 3 Stars | **Category:** tool

SOCIAL POPULARITY TOOL - http://kpmrs.com/social-popularity-tool.php

Enter your domain and this nifty tool will tell you if anyone has mentioned your URL on the social media web.

Rating: 3 Stars | **Category:** tool

CYFE - http://cyfe.com

Cyfe is an all-in-one dashboard that helps you monitor and analyze data found across your online services, including Google Analytics, Salesforce, AdSense, MailChimp, Amazon, Facebook, WordPress, Zendesk, and Twitter. It has many features including: pre-built widgets, custom data sources, real time reports, and data exports. Cyfe's website is very thorough, allowing you to use this tool flexibly and easily for all your marketing needs.

Rating: 3 Stars | **Category:** service

ADDICTOMATIC - http://addictomatic.com

Nifty way to enter your company name or keyword and view a 'snapshot' of what's buzzing across multiple popular sources. Most useful for monitoring online reputation, admittedly at a high level of generality.

Rating: 3 Stars | **Category:** tool

16

CONFERENCES

The original social media: *the Real World*. Attend a real-world social media marketing conference and network with other humans. How quaint! Here are our picks for the most informative social media conferences. Where better to learn about online media, than in the real world? (*Be sure to be live tweeting while you're there*).

Here are the best social media marketing conferences!

SOCIAL MEDIA WORLD - http://socialmediaexaminer.com/smmworld

Social Media Marketing World claims to be the world's largest social media marketing conference. Learn from top social media experts.

Rating: 5 Stars | **Category:** conference

SOCIAL MEDIA STRATEGIES SUMMIT (SMSS) - http://socialmediastrategiessummit.com/

Social Media Strategies Summit is a social media marketing conference focused on providing engaging and informative social media case studies and concepts from the industry's leading companies and thought leaders. Learn top trends and innovative thoughts in social media, customer analytics and content from the finest social media experts and social media consultants.

Rating: 4 Stars | **Category:** conference

SOCIAL TOOLS SUMMIT - http://socialtoolssummit.com

Tools, content, and other key concepts about social media. More focused on the technical aspects than some of the other shows.

Rating: 3 Stars | **Category:** conference

SOCIAL MEDIA WEEK - http://socialmediaweek.org

Social Media Week is a leading set of worldwide conferences that curates and shares the best ideas, innovations and insights about how social media and technology are changing business, society and culture around the world. SMW hosts conferences on six continents, including Europe, North America, South America, Africa, Australia and Asia. Each Week is individually organized and consists of dozens of local events in the organizing city.

Rating: 3 Stars | **Category:** conference

SOCIAL FRESH CONFERENCE - http://socialfreshconference.com

Social Fresh Conference occurs twice yearly, once on each coast. A two-day digital conference, it features a single track with all the attendees in the same room and all speakers on the same stage. Social Fresh Conference focuses on practical and actionable content. Featured speakers are on stage for 30 minutes or less, not an hour, diving deep on specific topics without all the fluff.

Rating: 3 Stars | **Category:** conference

INBOUND - http://www.inbound.com/

INBOUND fuels the passion that drives the most innovative and successful business leaders of our time. INBOUND's purpose is to provide the inspiration, education, and connections you need to transform your business. More for content marketing than for SEO, but since content is king...

Rating: 2 Stars | **Category:** conference

17

PUBLICATIONS

Social Media is hot. It's so hot that there are many new media outlets that cover the topic. Here are our picks for the most informative blogs and portals that cover the Social Media universe. Where better to learn about online media, than online?

Here are the best **free** publications and blogs on Social Media Marketing, ranked with the best first!

WebProNews - http://www.webpronews.com/

Comprehensive (overwhelmingly so) resource for news, information, and tips related to online business. Search engines, search engine optimization (SEO), search engine marketing (SEM), social media marketing, advertising, and online branding - all covered in overwhelming detail. Information overload, but it does cover SEO and social media.

Rating: 5 Stars | **Category:** portal

Social Media Examiner - http://socialmediaexaminer.com

The look and feel of this one is pretty hokey, but the content is very, very good. Social Media Examiner focuses very much on the marketing aspects of social media marketing.In fact, while Mashable is more about social media 'in general,' Social Media Examiner is more about 'social media marketing.'

Rating: 5 Stars | **Category:** portal

Social Media Today - http://www.socialmediatoday.com/

Portal and blog by journalists, online managers, and advertising professionals in for those working in PR, marketing, advertising, on social media and marketing. It covers all aspects of social media tools, platforms, companies and personalities from a global perspective. All content is contributed by members and curated by editorial staff.

Rating: 4 Stars | **Category:** portal

Social Times - http://socialtimes.com

Nick O'Neill's megasite on Social Media. Can you say 'information overload?' Now owned by AdWeek.

Rating: 3 Stars | **Category:** blog

Mashable - http://mashable.com/

Mashable was once arguably the leading portal and information site for social media news and events. However, here's the rub for social media marketers: Mashable is everything about everything in social media, and lacks a strong focus on the marketing side of it. It sorta kinda wants to be Buzzfeed, so it's going CONSUMER on us, sadly rather than MARKETER.

Rating: 1 Stars | **Category:** portal

www.ingramcontent.com/pod-product-compliance
Lightning Source LLC
Chambersburg PA
CBHW060448060326
40689CB00020B/4474